YOU'RE THE FACE PAINTER!?

2 BOOKS
IN 1

FACE PAINTING

THE GOOD, THE BAD, AND THE OH MY!

TAJ MARKALE

You're the Face Painter!?

and

Face Painting Secrets The Good, The Bad, and The Oh My!

Taj Markale

ISBN (Print Edition): 979-8-35093-534-9

ISBN (eBook Edition): 979-8-35093-535-6

YOU'RE THE FACE PAINTER!?

TAJ MARKALE

*Dedicated to my family and supporters
throughout the years*

PROLOGUE:

He stood in front of the mirror, studying his reflection closely. As a black male face painter, he was used to being the odd one out. His profession was seen as something only women and white men did, and he often had to work twice as hard to prove his worth. But he refused to let that stop him.

He had always been drawn to the art of face painting, the way he could use his skills to transform a person's appearance and bring joy to their day. It was a way for him to express his creativity and connect with people from all walks of life.

But it wasn't easy. He had faced discrimination and racism, both from clients who doubted his abilities and from fellow artists who didn't believe a black man had a place in their industry. But he didn't let that stop him. He pushed forward, determined to prove them all wrong.

Through his experiences, he discovered the power of representation and the importance of diversity in the arts. He realized that by being true to himself and his craft, he could inspire others to do the same.

This book is a testament to his journey as a black male face painter, filled with stories of triumphs and setbacks, of perseverance and passion. It is a celebration of his artistry, and a call for greater inclusivity and acceptance in the world of face painting.

INTRODUCTION:

Face painting is a popular form of entertainment that can be enjoyed by people of all ages, backgrounds, and income levels. However, the way in which it is embraced and practiced can vary greatly depending on the demographics of the people involved.

In lower-income demographics, face painting is often seen as a low-cost activity that can be enjoyed by children at community events such as fairs, carnivals, and block parties. Face painters may use simpler designs and cheaper materials to keep costs low, and may even offer their services for free in order to give back to the community. In these settings, face painting can be a fun and creative way for children to express themselves and feel a sense of joy and wonder.

In contrast, in more affluent demographics, face painting is often associated with more elaborate and intricate designs. Professional face painters may be hired for private events such as birthday parties, weddings, and corporate events, and may use high-quality, non-toxic paints and tools to create stunning works of art on their clients' faces. These designs may incorporate glitter, rhinestones, and other embellishments, and may be tailored to fit the specific theme or style of the event. You are more likely to receive a tip with these clients.

Despite these differences, however, the underlying appeal of face painting remains the same across all demographics. Whether you are a child in a low-income community or a millionaire attending a high-end event, face painting can be a fun, creative, and immersive experience that allows you to express yourself and tap into your imagination in a unique and exciting way.

CHAPTER 1:
MY BACKGROUND

Growing up in Dallas, Texas I lived in the same apartments for 20 years. This location was considered one of the rougher areas of the city. I grew up in the apartments known as Cherokee Village at the time, on the intersection of Jim Miller and Elam Road. This was located exactly across the street from E. B. Comstock Middle School where I attended my seventh and eighth grade years.

Over there, if you were looking for trouble, you would find it. There were 7 different apartment complexes within a one mile radius. This means that people would unite in groups as crews or cliques. If someone had an issue with someone from a different complex, you are expected to feel the same way. If you're not one of us, then you must be one of them.

I have always had a natural gift with the arts. I can remember in first grade drawing sneakers and Teenage Mutant Ninja Turtles. I would gift these pictures to my classmates and draw roses to give to girls. I continued practicing art and always stood out in my art classes. I was using shading techniques in coloring books before I knew what showing depth and value really was.

I left Fredrick Douglass Elementary and went to Maynard H Jackson Vanguard School. This was considered a better school than the four to sixth grade school assigned to my address. I learned some advanced techniques in the art classes there.

I actually had a desk in the principal's office facing the wall. I was expelled for behavior at the end of my first semester in fourth grade. This caused me to go to the school associated with my address. The school where everyone from where I lived attended.

This is where I experienced temptations and peer pressure that a child my age should never have to. I had people from the apartments where I lived trying convince me to smoke cigarettes and Black and Mild cigars in fourth grade. In fifth grade, those same people were now smoking marijuana. I believe that they got it from other siblings but I never yield to the temptations. I had never had a desire or curiosity to smoke anything. This made me stand out and set me apart. If anything, I would fight if the opportunity presented itself but I never did drugs. This is when I knew that I was different.

Now, I am enrolled in the school known as R.C Burleson. This was also a forth to sixth grade school. The behavior that I had exemplified at Maynard Jackson was more common and normal at R. C. Burleson. I finished two years and a semester there and went to E. B. Comstock to experience middle school. I had pretty good grades, so this allowed me to be placed into advanced placement classes. Now that I was close to completing my eight grade year, I was always known throughout the schools for my art. I had been in special classes called T.A.G., Talented and Gifted. My grades were good enough for me to apply for High Schools other than my assigned high school, H. Grady Spruce. I had the option of going to Townview Magnet School, Booker T. Washington, or Skyline High School. I missed the deadlines to apply for all schools.

I was called to the office by my school counselor assigned to me. This was a process that was done for every student to prepare us for the middle school to high school transition. She asked why I didn't apply for any of the schools mentioned above. I told her that I would just go to Spruce. She told me that she was not going to allow me to go to Spruce. She asked me where I wanted to go out of the three schools. I told her, Skyline. Since my grades were good, the counselor contacted some of my teachers and they wrote me letters of recommendation. She submitted my information and within 2 days she told me that my application had been accepted and that I was going to Skyline.

At this time, you had to select what was called a cluster; this is what you would like to study for all four years of high school. Since I was good at art, I selected Advertising and Design. Throughout my four years of high school, I had two teachers who taught my cluster subject, one for the ninth and tenth grades, and a second for the eleventh and twelfth grades.

I was in the top three of my Ad Design classes depending on the projects, if not the top two. It was easy to me and I got bored so I would talk and keep myself entertained, which led me to being sent to the correction offices a lot of times. I spent more time in in-house suspension in twelfth grade than any other grade. I was receiving college credits in high school but I never went to college.

I had grown tired of school and being in advanced placement classes had allowed me to gain my credits needed to graduate earlier than others. Once I found out that I didn't need certain classes to graduate, I stop doing their work.

I would have regular art classes' as well in high school and not have to do the assignments that the other students were assigned. The teacher would have me working on her personal assignments that she had to do throughout the school.

In addition, all throughout school and living in my community, I would always observe the environment, the interactions, the habits, and the limitations. I grew up in a two parent household, but most of my neighbors couldn't say the same. Watching my parents go to work every day and take care of their kids, this taught me how to handle responsibility and how to stay consistent. I always have kept some type of income, legal income. I could've sold drugs at any time because they were easily accessible. I chose a different route.

To be more detailed and paint a more vivid picture, just imagine a group of kids playing a game of football in a field located in their apartments. Now imagine a parking lot attached to that same field with a different group of guys but they are selling drugs to cars that would pull up and park where they were directed. They were selling crack to be more specific.

By living in that type of environment and seeing those things on a daily bases will make you numb to it. Seeing the rolls of money, flashy cars, gold teeth with diamonds attached to them, was fascinating as a kid. They were considered to be cool. They would buy all the kids ice cream when the ice cream trucks would come through the apartments, give us a few dollars to let them know if we saw the police, and teach us how to defend ourselves. After experiencing all of that, I still chose a different route.

The only art that I was producing at that time was the assignments that were required from school. Everyone knew me as the artist in my neighborhood. I was always respectful and well known. I would take the elderly trash to the dumpsters and they would give me a hand full of change or a dollar most times. I would always help them carry their groceries in their houses without them having to ask. It was a no brainer. I would call time out on the football game and everyone would see me go help the elderly.

I graduated high school May of 2002, and had a son March of 2003. I will say that he helped me so much to slow down and stay on the right tracks, as I grew to my later teens, the temptations of the streets became stronger. The wanting to have the money to impress girls or just to not want to be considered broke, the clothes, shoes, and club hopping, or being in Deep Ellum, (a strip of bars and clubs in Dallas, Texas) on Friday and Saturday nights.

I was introduced to face painting in 2013. My wife, but girlfriend at the time was a manager at a dental office. They were having a customer appreciation and had different activities for the customers to do. She asked me if I wanted to face paint for the event. I told her that I would try. While I was face painting, people were asking if I face painted for parties. I had never painted at a party before, but I told them yes. This is when a light bulb turned on. Next, I created cards and started researching face painting tutorials on YouTube University.

CHAPTER 2:
"YES, I'M THE FACE PAINTER"

Now, I am a black male face painter. I say it this way because it's very rare. I am like a unicorn in the face painting industry. Some clients are supportive and want to give me a chance because I am a black male face painter. My work ethic and quality are just as good as any other face painter. In fact, if you would compare, I am better than most. I say this because I have no limitations, I have a natural creativity, and I can paint anything that is requested. ANYTHING! I don't use a vision board because I like to paint something that has a special meaning to the client. It seems like I am forcing them to choose a design that I want to paint if I use a selection board.

As a black male raising four sons in Texas, I have always been interested in finding unique and creative ways to bond with my children. One activity that we have enjoyed together over the years is face painting.

Face painting is an art that has been around for centuries. It is a fun way to express oneself and showcase creativity. In Texas, face painting is a popular activity for events and parties. However, being a black male in Texas can come with its unique challenges when it comes to face painting. This book will explore what it is like to be a black male face painter in Texas, the challenges faced, and the joys experienced.

"You're the face painter!?" "Yes", I replied. "I'm the face painter." This question was asked to me when the client opened the door. It wasn't the question, but the way that it was asked. I had been asked this question many times but this particular time it stuck with me.

I could feel the energy shift as I walked into the house. All eyes were on me. I have never been one to like attention. When your face painting, be prepared for everyone to watch you work and wait to see *the big reveal. I asked where I would be setting up. Within 3 minutes I was ready to start painting. Through my peripheral vision I could see eyes and heads glance at me periodically. Thinking to myself, I must represent. I have to represent for male face painters, black face painters, and all face painters.*

At parties my first face is always the birthday person. I try to be a little more detailed on the guest of honor. About five to seven minutes later, I hold my mirror up, the birthday kid shows all its teeth. "I love it", as it smiles. The birthday kid gets up and turns around, all you hear are gasps, and all you see are smiles. I have showcased my skills and have proved that I am credible as a face painter, as a male face painter, as a black male face painter.

When you think of a face painter, we have been used to seeing middle aged Caucasian women. This is true. I came to change the narrative and show that not only can men face paint, but black man can as well. About fifty percent of my clients are Caucasian. I have had some of the best times with them. Most have used my services multiple times and referred me to friends. I appreciate all of them and their hospitality. I had never felt unwelcomed and I'm greeted at the front door with a smile.

CHAPTER 3:
GETTING STARTED

If you are interested in starting a career as a face painter here are a few steps you can take to get started:

1. *Learn the skills: Start by learning how to paint faces. You can do this by taking a course or workshop, or by practicing on your own. There are many resources available online that can help you learn the basics of face painting.*

2. *Build your kit: Invest in high-quality face paints, brushes, and other tools. Look for products that are specially designed for use on skin, and choose colors that are vibrant and long lasting.*

3. *Practice, practice, practice: The more you practice, the better you'll become. Set up a practice space in your home and invite friends and family to be your models. You can also volunteer to paint faces at local events, such as fairs or festivals, to gain experience, exposure and build your portfolio.*

4. *Build your portfolio: Take pictures of your work and create a portfolio to showcase your skills. This will be helpful when you start looking for gigs.*

5. *Network: Reach out to other face painters in your area and attend networking events to build connections. Consider joining a professional organization, such as the Face Painting Association, to connect with other face painters and stay up-to-date on industry news and trends.*

6. *Market yourself: Create a website or social media presence to showcase your artwork and make it easy for potential clients to find you. Consider offering discounts or promotions to attract new clients and build your reputation.*

Remember that building a successful career as a face painter takes time and effort. With dedication and hard work, however, you can turn your passion for art into a rewarding and fulfilling profession.

Getting started as a face painter can be daunting, especially as a black male in Texas. The first step is to research and learn the basics of face painting. This can be done by attending workshops, reading books, and watching online tutorials. Once you have a basic understanding of face painting, it is important to invest in quality face paints and brushes.

Face painting is an art form that dates back centuries and is used for various purposes such as cultural celebrations, rituals, and even theater productions. In recent years, face painting has become a popular activity at parties, festivals, and other events. It involves applying paint to a person's face or body to create designs, patterns, or images.

My first time face painting, I used some face paint that I found on the shelf at Wal-Mart. That didn't go very well. The cheaper paints are harder to blend and barely cover the skin. It felt like I was painting with watercolors. After doing a little research, I found a paint that I love and still use today which is, Snazaroo. Snazaroo has over 50 different colors or types of paint to select from. If used correctly, you can get the look or design that you want.

Be sure that you are using face paint. I was scheduled at one event and they had a second face painter but that face painter was set up with different acrylic paints. Acrylic paints are used for art, canvas art, murals, and so. I looked at her and said, "I hope you're not about to use that, are you?"

It was her first time face painting. I offered to take care of the customers while she went to go get actual face paint. As we sat at the six foot table, we had customers form a line. I painted three faces to her one and I knew that my experience was showing. I gave her a few pointers and showed her different techniques.

She was a white teenager, and I didn't hesitate to show her the ropes. This is how not to discriminate.

CHAPTER 4:
CUSTOMER SERVICE

Providing exceptional customer service as a male black face painter requires a combination of skills, including attention to detail, creativity, and communication. As a black man, it is important to be aware of any biases that customers may have and to approach each interaction with professionalism and warmth.

One key aspect of providing exceptional customer service is to listen carefully to the needs and preferences of the customer. This can involve asking questions about the type of design they want, the colors they prefer, and any other special requests they may have. Taking the time to understand the customer's needs will ensure that the final result is something that they will be happy with.

In addition to listening, creativity is an important part of being a successful face painter. This may involve creating new designs that are unique and visually stunning, or adapting existing designs to suit the customer's preferences. Being able to come up with creative solutions to challenges is a valuable skill that can help set you apart from other face painters.

Communication is also key when providing exceptional customer service. As a male black face painter, it is important to communicate clearly and confidently with customers, and to be sensitive to any cultural differences that may arise. This may involve explaining the process of face painting, discussing design options, or providing reassurance to nervous or hesitant customers.

Finally, it is important to be professional and courteous at all times, no matter the situation. This means showing up on time, being well-prepared with all necessary supplies, and maintaining a positive *attitude throughout the event. Providing exceptional customer service as a male black face painter requires a commitment to excellence, creativity, communication, and professionalism, all of which can help build a loyal customer base and lead to long-term success in this exciting and rewarding field.*

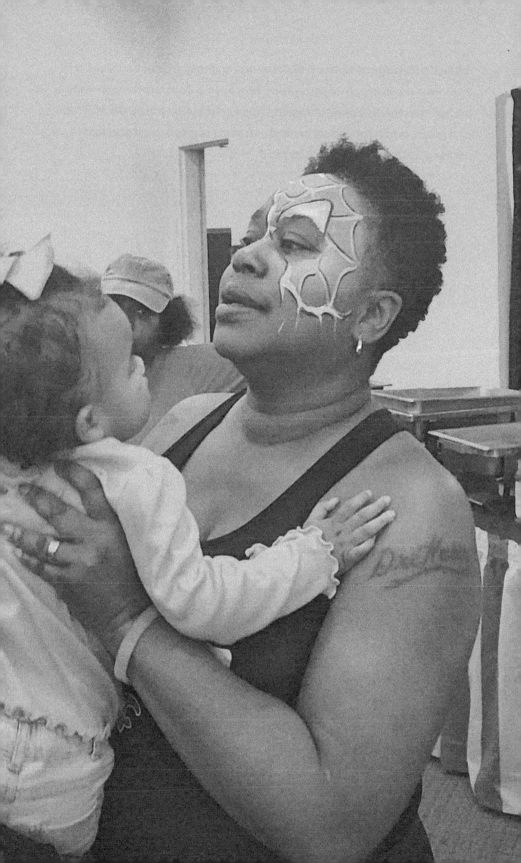

CHAPTER 5:
OVERCOMING STEREOTYPES
AND DISCRIMINATION

Unfortunately, face painting, like many activities, can be affected by stereotypes and discrimination. As a black male, I have experienced some negative reactions from others who do not expect me to be involved in face painting. Some clients may be hesitant to hire you because of their own biases and stereotypes. It is important to be prepared to address these biases and showcase your skills as a face painter. I have had the guest of client's watch me as I paint the first kid, and once I prove that I am credible, there are no more worries or stare downs. However, I have used these experiences as opportunities to educate others about the importance of diversity and inclusivity in all forms of art.

Also, as a male face painter, when I'm tagged for party request on social media, I sometimes don't get a response. I believe that maybe it's because women see me as a guy in their Messenger or (DM) Direct Messenger, and may feel that I am trying to show interest in them and not the party request. Women know that you can see when someone has read your message, so they don't read them at all. This causes me to miss an opportunity to face paint and them an opportunity to experience one of the best face painter's in Dallas.

I have experienced potential clients who reached out to me based on my photos and then all of a sudden just stop replying. I won't jump to any conclusions.

As a black face painter, my work has to stand out amongst the rest of the competition. My interaction with customers and conversation has to be top notch with five star communication, quality photo references, quick replies, and flexibility. A lot of customers want to see reviews before they hire you. Always ask customers could they leave you a review. If your services were worth their time, then they would be willing to leave you a review most of the time. After being a male, after being black, I am a face painter.

I have been the only black person at the event many of times. This hasn't bothered me because the crowd that I am celebrating with makes me feel welcomed and makes sure that I am comfortable. They check-in with me from time to time and introduce me to guest as they arrive. Prepare yourself to be hired for diverse atmospheres. You will be introduced to new types of food, music, dances, people, and celebrations.

It is unfortunate that in some parts of Texas, a white face painter may be hired before a black male face painter. This could be due to a variety of reasons, including biases, cultural norms, or even out-right discrimination.

It is important to acknowledge the historical and ongoing systemic racism and discrimination against black individuals in the United States. This discrimination has created barriers to education, employment, and other opportunities, which can make it more difficult for black individuals to compete for jobs, including in the face painting industry.

It is crucial for employers and individuals to actively work to address and eliminate these biases and discrimination in hiring practices. One way to do this is to actively seek out diverse candidates and to consider their qualifications and skills, rather than making assumptions based on their race or gender. Additionally, it is important to create a welcoming and inclusive work environment that value and respects diversity.

I was recently contacted by a representative on a Country Club in Plano, Texas. I have serviced multiple parties in that Plano, Frisco, and Parker. I know that my work is high-quality and my prices are competitive, if not lower than some of the competitions because I am a black male face painter. I'm not saying that my race had anything to do with it but, I have all five star reviews and my overall rating is five stars.

Please don't misunderstand me. I have had clients in Highland Park, Preston Hollow, Kennedale, Mansfield, Heath, Rockwall, Rowlett, Josephine, Fate, Waxahachie, Mesquite, Garland, Cedar Hill, Richardson, Farmers Branch, Irving, Bedford, Sunnyvale, and Dallas, Texas, and have not experienced any prejudices.

In conclusion, hiring decisions should be made solely based on qualifications and skills, rather than race and gender. It is time to break down these barriers and promote a more diverse and inclusive society, where everyone has equal access to opportunities, including in the face painting industry.

CHAPTER 6:
FINDING INSPIRATION

Inspiration can come from many sources, including nature, art, and culture. As a black male face painter in Texas, it may be helpful to draw inspiration from your own experiences and culture. This can help you stand out in a crowded industry and showcase your unique style and creativity.

Look for things that kids have heavy interest in, such as YouTube characters, animals, superheroes, and toys. When you are able to paint something that the kids love, they are able to cherish the moment more. You have created an everlasting memory. At the end of the day, my main goal is to make the kids smile when I hold my mirror up after the completion of their request.

As a natural artist, I look for inspiration everyday anywhere that I go. Artist can find inspiration in many different ways on a daily basis. Here are some common ways that artists look for inspiration:

1. Observing the world around them: Many artist find inspiration in the people, places, and objects they encounter in their daily lives. They might take a walk outside, people watch at a coffee shop, or explore a new part of town to spark their creativity.

2. Exploring other artists' work: Looking at the work of other artists can be a great source of inspiration. Artists might YouTube, online face painting communities, or watch certain movies to see what others are creating and to learn new techniques.

3. Trying new things: Sometimes, trying something new can be the key to unlocking inspiration. Artists might experiment to explore new creative avenues.

4. *Reflecting on personal experiences: Personal experiences and emotions can provide a wealth of inspiration for artist. They might journal, meditate, or talk to friends and family to process their feelings and gain insights that they can translate into their art.*

5. *Setting goals and challenges: Setting goals and challenges can help artists stay motivated and focused. They might challenge themselves on painting a certain number of faces in an hour, or try to paint a face in a new style or with a specific theme.*

Overall, finding inspiration is a deeply personal process, and what works for one artist may not work for another. It's important for artists to experiment with different methods and find what works best for them.

CHAPTER 7:
EXPANDING YOUR SKILLS

As a face painter, it is important to continually expand your skills and knowledge. This can be done by attending workshops, learning new techniques, and experimenting with different styles. Don't forget YouTube University. As a black face painter in Texas, it may be helpful to seek out mentors and other professionals who can provide guidance and support. I am willing to mentor those who have a passion for the art.

Having an art background can be extremely beneficial when it comes to face painting, as it provides a solid foundation in color theory, composition, and design. Here are some tips for using your art background to improve your face painting skills.

1. **Color Theory:** Your knowledge of color theory will come in handy when choosing colors for your designs. You'll know which colors work well together and how to create different shades and tones.

2. **Composition:** Understanding composition will help you create balanced and visually pleasing designs. You'll know how to create a focal point and how to balance out the rest of the design.

3. **Design:** Having a background in design will help you create unique and creative face painting designs. You'll be able to create intricate patterns and designs that stand out.

4. **Technique:** Your art background will give you a foundation in various techniques such as blending, shading, and highlighting. These skills will help you create realistic and dimensional designs.

Remember, practice makes better! Keep practicing your face painting skills and continue to use your art background to create unique and beautiful designs.

CHAPTER 8:
BUILDING A BUSINESS

Building a successful face painting business takes time and effort. It is important to have a strong online presence, network with other professionals in the industry, and consistently showcase your work. As a black male face painter in Texas, it may be helpful to connect with other black professionals in the industry and leverage their support and mentorship.

You must pass a background check. I want to keep kids safe. When using apps to find jobs this will be a requirement to be an employee or partner with most apps. This is another reason why I got into face painting. I wanted to show a strong male presence having fun with kids and being a positive influence and role model.

Step away from the television, research, and only get on social media if you are looking for face painting jobs or posting your work. Facebook has a lot of party groups where potential customers post request for face painters and more.

A close friend of mine by the name of Toya Walker created the party group, DFW Party Resource on Facebook. This group has over 16k members. I have been hired for parties from the group multiple times. For every event or party that you serve, you have potential customers. Never leave a party or event without passing out cards or some type of way for people to contact you. This is imperative.

At times, you will be asked to be a vendor for events. Being a vendor has its pros and cons. You may pay to be a vendor and only paint five faces, you may have a profitable day, or you may leave in the negative. One thing that would be positive is that you got exposure and networking connects and gained vendor experience.

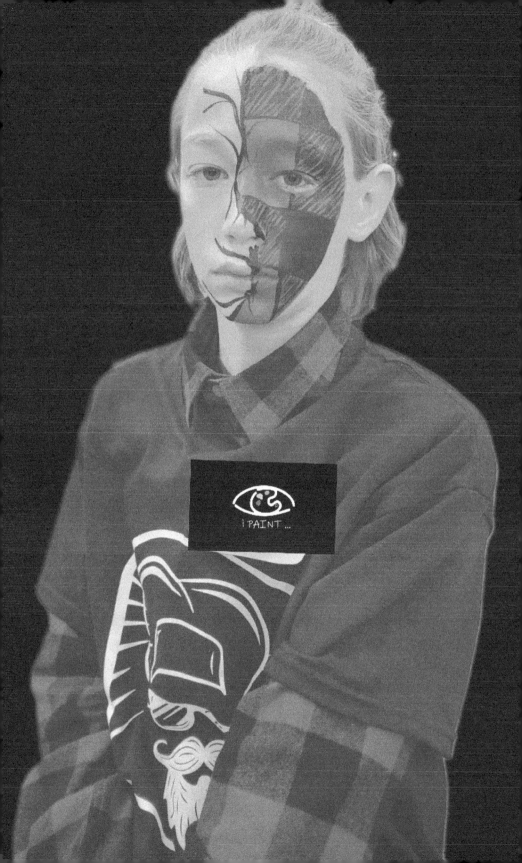

CHAPTER 9:
SHOWCASING YOUR SKILLS

As a face painter, your work speaks for itself. It is important to consistently showcase your skills and creativity to attract new clients and retain current ones. This can be done through social media, in-person events, and online portfolios.

The number of faces a face painter can paint per hour depends on several factors, such as the complexity of the designs, the skill level of the face painter, and the age of the participants. However, a professional face painter can typically paint 10 to 20 faces per hour.

Simple designs, such as a basic butterfly or spider, can be painted quickly and efficiently, while more complex designs, such as a full-face superhero or animal, may take longer. Additionally, young children may require more time and patience from the face painter, as they may move around or be afraid of the process.

Overall, the number of faces a face painter can paint per hour varies depending on the circumstances, but a range of 10 to 20 per hour is a good estimate for a professional face painter.

Never stop being creative. I allow my clients to select whatever comes to their imagination. This helps me better myself, add more designs to my muscle memory, standout when compared to other face painters, and verify that they have hired the right person. Not limiting myself allows me to remain creative and showcase my skills.

I recommend using stencils for animal prints or small designs that will take more time if painted by free hand. As an artist, I don't like to use them, but if I'm making animal prints it does speed up the process.

CHAPTER 10:
COLLABORATING WITH OTHER ARTIST

Collaborating with other artists can be a great way to expand your skills and grow your business. This can be done by working on joint projects, attending industry events, and participating in online forums. As a black male face painter in Texas, it may be helpful to collaborate with other black professionals in the industry to promote diversity and inclusivity.

I have been hired for big events with thousands of people and had to work side by side with other face painters. I was asked if I could only paint certain designs. I told the lady, "No". If I had only painted limited designs, it wouldn't allow me to showcase my skills and stand out as a black male face painter. Being in the 1 percentile, I need to be better than good to attract customers and receive party request.

Collaborating with other face painters can be an incredibly rewarding experience, especially as a black male face painter. Despite the challenges that may come with being a minority in the industry, working with others who share a love for the art of face painting can lead to valuable learning opportunities, networking connections, and a sense of community.

As a black male painter, it's important to find other artists who value diversity and inclusivity in their work. Collaborating with like-minded individuals who share a passion for creating beautiful, culturally sensitive designs can help to break down barriers and promote greater understanding and appreciation for different cultures and perspectives.

In addition to the artistic benefits of collaboration, working with other face painters can also lead to opportunities for professional growth and development. By sharing ideas, techniques, and resources with others, you can expand your skill set, increase your exposure to new markets, and build a stronger reputation within the industry.

Of course, collaborating with other face painters can also be challenging at times. There may be differences in artistic styles, approaches, or business practices that need to be navigated in order to achieve a successful partnership. However, by focusing on clear communication, mutual respect, and a share commitment to creating quality work, these challenges can be overcome.

Ultimately, collaborating with other face painters as a black male artist can be an incredibly rewarding experience. By working together to create beautiful, culturally sensitive designs, we can help to promote greater understanding, diversity, and inclusivity within the face painting community and beyond.

CHAPTER 11:
PRICING

The average cost of face painting in Texas can vary depending on several factors, such as the location, the type of event, the experience of the face painter, and the complexity of the designs.

However, the average cost of face painting in Texas ranges from $100 to $200 per hour. Some face painters may charge an hourly rate, while others may charge per face or per event. Depending on the location, I would not take a one hour job unless I needed it at the moment. Choose your jobs and locations wisely.

It's essential to research and compare the prices of different face painters in your area to find the best one that fits your budget and needs. Additionally, some face painters may offer discounts for larger events or longer hours.

You can check the average price of your competitors online by using Google. I do recommend that you request a deposit when being booked for reservations. Also, always ask and take into consideration the number of customers that you will have, this will help when pricing. Sell it to the customer that they are only paying $5 per face or what have you.

You can grow your portfolio by parting for free at family gatherings, practicing on friends, or even painting on yourself. Take as many photos as possible and pick the best. Always edit before posting online.

People will try to lowball you if you let them. They will mention the ages of the kids, or that they don't want the full face, and even say things like every kid may not get their face painted. Set you price and stick with it. I sometimes offer discounts to repeat customers. You'll be surprised that even with your set price; people will still tip you afterwards.

However, prices can vary widely depending on the individual artist and their experience level. Some may charge more if they have won awards or have a high-profile client list, while others may offer lower rates for a basic service.

Compared to the rest of the United States, the pricing of a 2-hour face painting service in Texas is generally in line with the national average. According to a survey by Thumbtack, a platform that connects customers with local service providers, the average cost for face painting services across the country ranges from $75 to $150 per hour. This means that a 2-hour service in Texas falls within the national average, though it may be slightly higher or lower depending on the specific artist and location.

Ultimately, the pricing of a 2-hour face painting service in Texas versus the United States can vary depending on a number of factors. It is important for clients to research and compare different artists and their pricing to find a service that fits their budget and meets their needs.

CHAPTER 12:
FINDING AND ACCEPTING JOBS

ere are some general tips on how to find and accept face painting jobs:

1. **Build a portfolio:** Create a portfolio of your previous face painting work. You can showcase your portfolio on your website or social media accounts.

2. **Network:** Attend events where face painting may be in demand, such as festivals, birthday parties, and corporate events. Hand out business cards and network with people who may be interested in hiring you.

3. **Advertise:** Promote your face painting services online through social media platforms like Facebook, Instagram, and Twitter. You can also place ads in local newspapers or on community bulletin boards.

4. **Offer discounts:** Offer discounts for the first-time customers or for a referrals to help build your clientele.

5. **Respond promptly:** When you receive an inquiry about your services, respond promptly and professionally to show your interest in the job.

6. **Be flexible:** Be willing to work flexible hours, including weekends and evenings, to accommodate clients' schedules

7. **Keep records:** Keep a record of your bookings, payments, and expenses to help you manage your business effectively.

Remember that building a successful face painting business takes time and effort, so be patient and persistent in your efforts to find and accept jobs. As a black male face painter, I still hesitate to take jobs in certain locations because I don't feel safe in the area or just want to avoid a possibility of interaction with law enforcement. This a big concern sometimes being a father of four son's.

One of my most memorable jobs was a home located in Highland Park. I arrived at the home and there were three people outside. I lowered my window to verify the address and to announce that I was the face painter, and they asked me did I want to self-park or valet. I chose to self-park because I didn't have cash at the time. This was a first; I had never been to a party where they had valet service. This wasn't the wow factor. When I walked to the backyard I saw an extravagant setup. This customer had hired two face painters, a magician, jugglers, a party character, and catering. This was not your average party. Also, I didn't mention the photographer.

Being hired as a face painter at million dollar homes can be an interesting and lucrative job opportunity. Face painting is a form of art that can transform a person's appearance and make them look like anything they want. It is especially popular among children who enjoy being transformed into their favorite animals, superheroes, or princesses.

If you are a skilled face painter, then you may be able to find work in high-end neighborhoods where people are willing to pay top dollar for quality entertainment. These affluent areas often have lavish homes with large backyards that are perfect for hosting events like birthday parties, weddings, and other special occasions.

When working at million dollar home, it's important to be professional and reliable. You will be workings in a high-end environment, so you need to make sure that you're dressed appropriately and that your equipment is clean and well-maintained. You should also arrive on time and be prepared to work for the duration of the event.

One of the perks of working at million dollar homes is that you may be able to charge higher rates than you would at other events. The people who live in these areas are used to paying top dollar for quality services, so they may be willing to pay more for your face painting skills. Additionally, you may be able to build a network of clients who will recommend you to their friends and family, leading to more opportunities for work.

When working at these events, it's also important to be flexible and adaptable. You may be asked to work in a variety of settings, such as indoors or outdoors, and you may need to adjust your painting techniques to fit the preferences of different clients. It's also important to be patient and friendly, as children can be unpredictable and may need extra attention to sit still for their face painting session.

Being hired as a face painter at million dollar homes can be a rewarding and profitable job opportunity for skilled artists. It requires professionalism, reliability, flexibility, and adaptability to work in these high-end environments, but potential for high pay and networking opportunities can make it a great choice for artists looking to expand their client base.

Face painting can be a fun and engaging for children and families in lower income communities, and can provide an opportunity for creativity and self-expression. However, it is important to consider accessibility and affordability of materials.

One approach to providing face painting in lower income communities could be to partner with local community organizations or schools to organize face painting events or workshops. This could involve sourcing affordable and safe face painting materials, such as water-based paints and brushes, and providing training and guidance on how to use them safely and effectively.

In conclusion, in lower income communities from my experience, you will be painting more kids. I suggest that you use smaller designs and have a limited amount of kids that you can paint. Always delivery quality work, because you are still representing your brand or your name. Most requests for services will come from someone who has seen your work. Remember that you are working with kids. Regardless of the surroundings or the environment, the kids still deserve to experience face painting services and leave the chair with a smile.

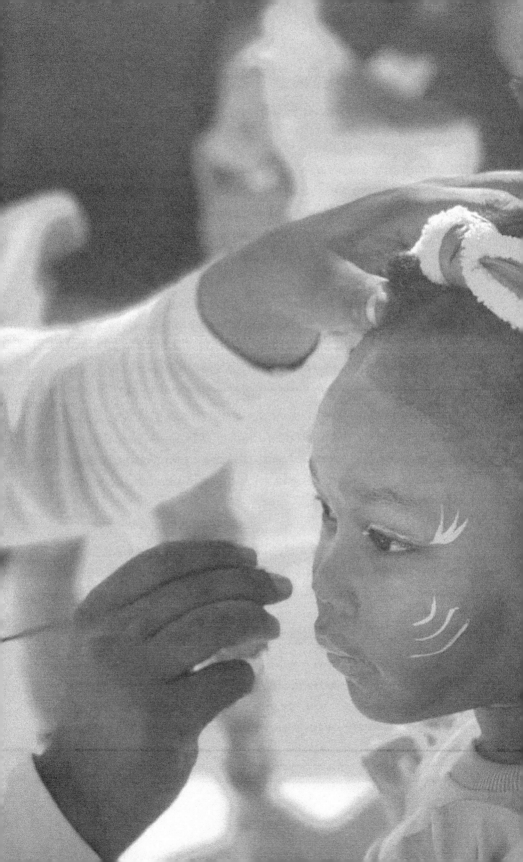

CHAPTER 13:
EVENTS

Setting up at events as a vendor selling face painting services, can be an exciting and rewarding experience. As a face painter, you have the opportunity to bring joy and creativity to children and adults alike, as you transform their faces into works of art. However, setting up for these events can be a bit of a challenge, and it requires careful planning and preparation.

Before the event, it's important to make sure that you have all the necessary supplies and equipment. This includes paints, brushes, sponges, water, cups, and anything else that you might need to create your designs. You'll also need to bring a table, chairs, and a tent or canopy to provide shade and shelter from the sun or rain.

Once you arrive at the event, you'll need to find a suitable spot to set up your booth. This should be a high-traffic area where the people can easily see and approach you. It's also a good idea to decorate your booth with balloons, signs, and other eye-catching decorations to attract attention.

When the event begins, be prepared for a busy and fast-paced day. You'll need to work quickly and efficiently paint as many faces as possible, while still providing each customer with a high-quality and unique design. It's important to be friendly and engaging with your customers, as this will help to build a good reputation and attract repeat business.

Overall, setting up at events as a face painting vendor can be a fun and rewarding experience. By following these tips and providing high-quality services, you can make a name for yourself in the face painting community and bring joy to many people through your artistic creations.

To be honest I stick out to potential clients because I'm not your average idea of a face painter. I play music and use lights to draw attention. I have seen other face painting vendors use online photos as their promotion, photos that were not their work. I wouldn't recommend this, because people will expect that same type of quality. This may be necessary for those who haven't created muscle memory.

Also, one experience that I had at a wedding while I was painting a little girl. Her mom walked to my side of the table even though my back was against the wall, and leaned her head on my shoulder as I painted her daughter. I later found out that her husband was at the wedding as well. This was a white woman. I believe that maybe her husband was looking at the women at the wedding, and she was trying to get back at him.

If I'm not mistaking, I think that the husband walked up and looked at his daughter's face and right before and turned and walked away, he looked at his wife. Like I stated earlier, I saw all of this through my peripheral vision. I was speechless and confused at the same time. I wasn't sure if she was amazed by the face painting, or the face painter.

CHAPTER 14:
CLEANING YOUR EQUIPMENT

When it comes to cleaning your equipment, I recommend using common household products. There is no need to purchase Jerry's Brush Cleaner, or Dan's Disinfectant. I use common household products, dish soap and alcohol. I start by rinsing the used sponges and paint brushes with warm water.

Next, I squeeze dish soap all over the products and massage them in the sponges by squeezing and releasing, and inside the brushes by using my fingers. Once they are all soapy I rinse them with warm water. If I need to repeat the process with the dish soap a second time, I repeat until no paint is dripping from the item when squeezed.

After, I have rinsed the sponges and brushes; I pour alcohol on them and squeeze the excess alcohol out of the item. Lastly, I let the items air dry. Be sure to reshape your brushes into the shape that they were purchased. This will help maintain the life of the brushes.

In my opinion, red paint is the most difficult to clean out of your brushes. It has been multiple times that I thought that I cleaned my brush thoroughly, but when I was trying to use white on a face, the paint was pink when I tested a stroke on myself and the client.

In addition to cleaning your brushes and sponges after each use, it's also important to regularly sanitize your palette, containers, and any other tools or equipment you use. You can use alcohol wipes or a solution of water and rubbing alcohol to disinfect these items.

CHAPTER 15:
PACE YOURSELF

As an hourly face painter, it is important to pace yourself in order to ensure that you are able to provide quality face painting services throughout the entire duration of your scheduled time. Here are some tips to help you pace yourself:

1. *Plan your time: Before starting, make sure you have a clear understanding of how many faces you need to paint and how much time you have. This will help you plan how long you can spend on each face.*

2. *Stick to a routine: Develop a routine that works for you and stick to it. This will help you stay organized and work efficiently.*

3. *Take breaks: Take short breaks every hour to rest your hands and avoid burnout. Use this time to stretch, hydrate, and refocus.*

4. *Use efficient techniques: Use efficient painting techniques that allow you to cover large areas quickly without compromising the quality of your work.*

5. *Communicate with clients: Communicate with the clients about the time it will take to paint each face and manage their expectations accordingly.*

Remember, pacing yourself is key to providing quality face painting services and ensuring customer satisfaction. You will get tired depending on the difficulty of the face that you are painting. Holding your arms up for hours can be a workout. Leaning and twisting will have you feeling sore the next morning. I try to turn my chair so that the client is facing the party or celebration, this way it will alleviate any movement from the client. People like to watch the process. I also try to keep the client's face at shoulder level. This eliminates any overextending and reaching for the clients. If I am painting an adult, I may stand so that I don't have to reach up. I sit as I paint, most of the time. By sitting and painting, it puts me face-to-face or eye level with most kids.

You'll have some people who want to talk the entire time. You'll have the people who want to look at every movement. You'll have the person who wasn't finished eating and gets in the chair still chewing. You'll have your scratcher. You'll have the siblings that fight to be the first to get their face painted. I always select the youngest first in that type of situation. You'll have the adults that just want to get anything as they sit in the chair with a drink in their hand.

You'll have the crying kid that you know doesn't want their face painted but the parent is trying to force them. In this situation, I always take a clean brush and rub it across their hand. Depending on how they react to it, I may try my second step which is rub the brush on their face. If this doesn't work, my last two methods are giving them a brush to let them try to paint me, or ask the parent to hold the mirror so that they can see me painting their face. This works most of the time.

You'll have the latecomers to show up ten to fifth-teen minutes before your time is about to expire. I may paint them, but that's if I'm not booked for another job. Also, it depends on how I'm feeling. I had to learn to say no. I created a sign to notify customers who is the last person in line. We must say no, because at an event people will con-tinue to get in line and your day will never end. Sometimes kids will cry but we can't always have everything that we desire. You'll also have kids who were there before everyone else, but they wait until you have started packing up to leave and want a face painting. This is when quality doesn't matter to me anymore.

CHAPTER 16:
THE JOY OF FACE PAINTING

The joy of face painting comes from seeing the smiles on my clients' faces and the creativity that comes from the art form. Face painting can be a truly joyful and exciting experience for both children and adults alike. The ability to transform oneself into a character, animal, or object with the stroke of a brush and the use of colorful paints is both creative and fun.

There are many reasons why face painting can bring joy. For children, it can be a way to express their imaginative and creativity. They can become their favorite superhero, princess, or animal, and feel like they are truly embodying that character. This can also be a fun activity for children's parties or events, as they can all have their faces painted together and play games or engage in other activities while dressed up.

For adults, face painting can also be a way to tap into their creativity and have some fun. It can be away to escape from the stress of daily life and feel like a kid again. Additionally, face painting can be a fun way to express oneself and show off one's personality at events like festivals, concerts, or even Halloween parties.

Moreover, the act of face painting can also be a source of joy for the artist themselves. As they create each design, they can feel a sense of satisfaction and accomplishments as they bring their vision to life. Seeing the smiles on their clients' faces and the joy that their art brings can also be incredibly rewarding.

Overall, face painting can be a wonderful and joyful experience for both the painter and the person being painted. It allows for self-expression, creativity, and fun, and can bring a sense of childlike wonder to any occasion.

One of my favorite parts of celebrating with people by face painting, is that you get offered food and drinks most of the time. Some client's will insist that you take a break and eat or ask that you take some food to go. I'm not one to turn down a free meal. Especially, after you've been painting and smelling the food the entire time, you haven't ate anything since breakfast, and you just watch someone take a bite of food and watch it fall on the plate. Of course, you see this through your peripheral vision. Although, your mouth is watering, your hands must be painting.

The only thing that I never do is accept an alcoholic beverage of any kind while I am painting. If I do accept one, I do so after I have completely finished and packed up my equipment. You don't want a photo of you going around the internet and become a meme as the drunk face painter. Even though I believe that my client's wouldn't do anything like that, people are always looking for a way to go viral. I don't want to be on the wrong end of the meme. My logo is noticeable and I am too by being a black, male, face painter.

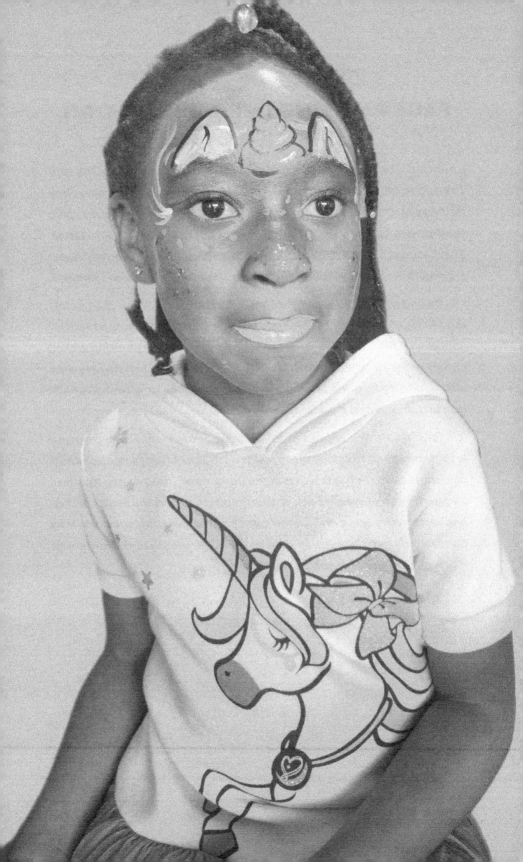

CHAPTER 17:
FACE PAINTING DURING INFLATION

Inflation occurs when the general level of prices for goods and services increases, while the purchasing power of the currency decreases. During inflation, face painting artists in Texas may raise their prices to keep up with the rising cost of materials and labor. This can make it difficult for families to afford face painting services, especially if they have multiple children who want their faces painted.

During a recession, on the other hand, the demand for face painting services may decrease as families cut back on non-essential spending. This can lead to a decrease in prices as face painting artists compete for a smaller pool of customers. However, artists may also struggle to make ends meet during a recession as they face a reduction in demand and a decrease in income.

To mitigate the impact of inflation and recession, face painting artists may need to find ways to reduce costs or offer promotions and discounts to attract customers. Face painting in Texas during inflation and recession presents both challenges and opportunities for artists and customers alike. While the cost of face painting services may fluctuate during these economic conditions, the joy and excitement it brings to children remain constant.

CHAPTER 18:
BECOMING A 5 STAR FACE PAINTER

Positive feedback from clients: One of the best ways to know if you're a great face painter is by receiving positive feedback from clients. If clients consistently praise your work, refer you to others, book you for repeat events, it's a good sign that you're doing something right.

Consistently producing high-quality work: Another sign that you're a great face painter is by consistently producing high-quality work. This means that your designs are creative, well-executed, and use high-quality products that last for the duration of the event.

Keep up with the latest trends: A great face painter stays up-to-date with the latest trends in the industry, including new designs, techniques, and products. By staying current, you can offer clients a wide range of options and keep your work fresh and exciting. You can also do this by staying current with movies and new YouTube characters.

Be efficient and organized: A great face painter is efficient and organized, able to work quickly while still producing quality work. This means having all your supplies organized and ready to go, being able to manage your time effectively during events.

Constantly seek to improve: Finally, a great face painter is always seeking to improve their skills. This means taking classes and workshops, practicing new designs, and seeking feedback from clients and other professionals in the industry.

By focusing on these areas and constantly striving to improve, you can become a great face painter and continue to grow your skills and reputation in the industry.

Crating muscle memory wit face painting ideas can be a fun and exciting way to improve your skills and develop your technique. Here are some tips for creating muscle memory with face painting ideas:

1. *Practice regularly: The key to creating muscle memory is to practice regularly. Set aside some time each day or week to work on your face painting skills. The more you practice, the more your muscles will remember the movements and techniques required to create the designs you want.*

2. *Start with simple designs: When you're first starting out, it's important to start with simple designs. This will help you to build your skills and develop your technique. Once you've mastered the basics, you can move on to more complex designs.*

3. *Break down the design: When you're working on a new design, break it down into smaller parts. This will help you to focus on each individual element and develop your muscle memory for each movement.*

4. *Use reference materials: Reference materials like books, videos, and online tutorials can be a great way to learn new techniques and develop your muscle memory. Study the materials closely and practice the techniques until you feel comfortable with them.*

5. *Experiment with different tools: Experimenting with different tools like brushes, sponges, and stencils can help you to develop your muscle memory for different techniques. Try using different tools to achieve different effects and see what works best for you.*

By following these tips, you can develop your muscle memory for face painting and create stunning designs with ease. Remember, practice makes better, so keep practicing and experimenting to improve your skills over time.

If you believe that you have provided five star service, don't hesitate to ask the client for a review. It is always better if they personalize it by including your name. Some clients will only hire you based on your reviews, and then your work. They don't care about your race.

CONCLUSION

In conclusion, this book has shed light on the experience of being a black male face painter. Through the lens of the author's personal journey, readers have gained a deeper understanding of the challenges and triumphs that come with pursuing a career in this unique and creative field. The author's voice has been a powerful testament to the importance of representation and diversity in the arts, and his story has inspired readers to pursue their own passions with courage and conviction.

Throughout the book, we have seen how the author's identity as a black man has both shaped and been shaped by his experiences as a face painter. From encountering discrimination and stereotypes to discovering new avenues for self-expression, the author's journey has been a testament to the resilience and creativity of the human spirit. By sharing his story, the author has not only given voice to the struggles of black male face painters or even male face painters, but he has also provided a roadmap for others who may be facing similar challenges in their own lives.

Ultimately, this book is a celebration of the power of art to connect us to ourselves and to one another. Through his work as a face painter, the author has brought joy and wonder to countless individuals, and he has remained us all of the transformative power of imagination and creativity. This book is a testament to the importance of diversity and inclusion in all aspects of life, and it serves as a powerful reminder that every voice deserves to be heard and every story deserves to be told.

EPILOGUE:

As the final stroke of paint was applied to the last child's cheek, the face painter sat back, exhausted but exhilarated. This had been his busiest day yet, and he was already looking forward to the next event where he could bring joy to more children.

As the pages of "You're the Face Painter" come to a close, the story of a black male face painter reaches its end. Throughout the book, the reader was taken on a journey through the experiences, triumphs, and challenges of this skilled artist.

From the very beginning, it was clear that the protagonist was not your typical face painter. As a black male, he often faced discrimination and stereotypes in the predominately white and female-dominated industry. However, he refused to let these obstacles deter him from pursuing his passion.

Through hard work and dedication, the face painter built a thriving business, earning a reputation for his unique and creative designs, His customers were diverse, ranging from children's parties to corporate events. Over time, he had become a sought-after face painter, known for intricate designs and attention to detail.

But the road was not always smooth. The artist faced moments of doubt, wondering if his race and gender would prevent him from truly succeeding in his chosen field. He also grappled with balancing his artistic pursuits with his responsibilities as a father and husband.

But more than that, he had become a role model for other black males who were interested in pursuing a career in the arts, He had shown them that it was possible to succeed, even in an industry that wasn't always welcoming to people who looked like him.

As he packed up his supplies and headed home, the face painter knew that he had found his calling. He was proud to be a face painter, and even prouder to be a black male face painter. He had proven that no matter who you are or where you come from, you can achieve your dreams if you work hard and never give up.

FACE PAINTING
SECRETS

THE GOOD, THE BAD, AND THE OH MY!

TAJ MARKALE
IPAINTBYTAJ

Dedicated to those connected to me in any way

INTRODUCTION

Welcome to the second edition of "Face Painter Secrets: The Good, The Bad, and The Oh My!" In this heartfelt and unfiltered account, we delve into the experiences of a black male face painter, exposing the raw truth that lies behind the captivating artistry. Through these pages, you will witness a deeper version of the face painter's perspective, one that unveils the untold stories and unveils the complex layers of this incredible journey.

When the first edition of "You're the Face Painter" was released, it opened the door to the colorful world of face painting, inviting readers to explore the magic and joy that is born from the brushstrokes of imagination. However, as the author, I felt compelled to bring forth a more honest and vulnerable narrative—a narrative that transcends the surface, delving into the intricacies faced by a black male artist in a predominantly white industry.

This second edition is a testament to the power of storytelling, the cathartic release that comes from sharing our truths, and the impact our experiences can have on others. Within these pages, you will find a collection of anecdotes, revelations, and reflections that illuminate the unique challenges, triumphs, and lessons learned throughout my journey as a black male face painter.

Prepare to embark on a rollercoaster of emotions. I will lay bare the good, the moments that fill the heart with warmth and reaffirm the beauty of this craft. I will expose the bad, the encounters marred by prejudice, discrimination, and the struggle to navigate through an industry that still grapples with diversity and inclusion. And finally, I will unravel the "Oh My!" moments, those unexpected twists and turns that force us to question, to grow, and to forge a path beyond the limitations imposed upon us.

This second edition is an invitation to break down barriers and ignite conversations. It's an opportunity to shed light on the untold stories and experiences that too often remain hidden in the shadows. It is my hope that by sharing these secrets, we can challenge perceptions, dismantle stereotypes, and inspire change within the face painting community and beyond.

So, come with me as we peel back the layers, uncover the untold narratives, and embrace the power of authenticity. Let us explore the multifaceted world of face painting through the lens of a black male artist, discovering the truths that lie beneath the vibrant façade. Together, we will navigate the good, the bad, and the "Oh My!" moments, forging a path towards a more inclusive and understanding future.

Welcome to "Face Painter Secrets: The Good, The Bad, and The Oh My!" Prepare to be moved, enlightened, and inspired.

TAJ MARKALE

CHAPTER 1:
ADAPTIVE BEHAVIOR

Adaptive behaviors include life skills such as grooming, dressing, working, money management, cleaning, making friends, social skills, and the personal responsibility expected of their age, social group and wealth group.

I grew up in what some would consider to be the "hood". I talk about this in my first book, "You're the Face Painter". I saw guys selling drugs on an everyday bases. I remember walking outside one day and my neighbor was standing in the corner of the next building. He was holding a soda can in his hand and I was seeing smoke come from the top of it. As he was talking to me, he would place a lighter under it and inhale the smoke from the can. He was smoking crack.

Everyone around the neighborhood would call me T, or Mr.T as a nickname. The name Mr. T came from the guy with all the chains around his neck on the television show, The A-Team. He said to me, "T, you not gone get out here and make you some of this money man? They're over there eating. Young guy like yourself, might as well get you a little change in your pocket". I said, "No, I'm good". This was a slang term. It means nothing other than, I am content with my current situation. Also, the term eating, refers to making money or an abundant profit according to the current demographics.

Although it was tempting, I never yielded to the temptation. I grew up with guys that were selling drugs in elementary school. Like I stated in my first book, some were also smoking in fourth and fifth grades as well. I never yielded to the temptation. I never had a desire and I saw what the cause and effects were of participating in those types of activities.

As a black male face painter, having adaptive behavior is essential to succeeding in the industry. Not only does it help with attracting and retaining customers, but it also increases the likelihood of securing more gigs. Adaptability is the ability to adjust to new situations, environments, and people in a way that is both effective and respectful. As a black male face painter, it is important to have this skill set to succeed in a highly competitive and ever-changing industry.

One of the most important aspects of having adaptive behavior as a black male face painter is being able to connect with customers from diverse backgrounds. Face painting is an activity enjoyed by people of all ages and cultures, so it is important to have the ability to communicate effectively with people from different walks of life. This includes being able to understand and respect different cultural customs and traditions that may be present at events.

Being adaptable also means having the ability to adjust your style of face painting to meet the needs and preferences of your clients. Every customer is unique and may have a specific idea of what they want their face painting design to look like. Having the ability to adjust your style and approach based on their preferences is crucial for providing a positive customer experience. This can also lead to more business through word of mouth referrals from satisfied customers.

Adaptive behavior also helps with seeking gigs as a black male face painter. It is important to be able to market yourself in a way that is both professional and approachable. Being able to adjust your approach based on the event and the audience can make a significant difference in how potential clients perceive you. For example, if you are painting faces at a children's birthday party, you may need to approach parents and children in a more playful and lighthearted manner. Conversely, if you are painting faces at a corporate event, a more professional and polished approach may be necessary.

Another aspect of adaptive behavior that can help with seeking gigs is having the ability to anticipate and adapt to changes in the industry. This includes staying up-to-date on new face painting techniques and products, as well as being aware of emerging trends in the industry. By staying ahead of the curve, you can position yourself as a knowledgeable and skilled professional in the industry, which can lead to more gig opportunities.

If you were to hold a conversation with me or pick my brain, you wouldn't be able to tell that I came from where I came from. This is why I know that I could be effective with kids that have experienced the same things or with teens of this day and age. I have proven myself to be worthy. I didn't indulge in activities that could affect my future so I never caught a case, which means that my record was and is clean. If I would've kept that same energy and stayed with the mind frame of the "hood", I would never have the customers and be trusted with my customer's kids.

Also, although I am a black male face painter, I don't only target black clients. I like to have a diverse customer rapport. Being able to speak correctly and properly helps me with gaining diverse clientele. Having a limited method of communication will limit my financial opportunities and growth. Remember this, Coca Cola advertises to all, not just a certain type even though it is a product and not a service.

In conclusion, having adaptive behavior as a black male face painter is essential for success in the industry. It helps with attracting and retaining customers, as well as seeking out new gigs. By being able to connect with customers from diverse backgrounds, adjust your style and approach based on their preferences, market yourself effectively, and stay up-to-date on industry trends, you can position yourself as a highly skilled and sought-after face painter.

CHAPTER 2:
FACE PAINTING AS A
LUCRATIVE ART FORM

Introduction: Throughout our journey in exploring the realm of art, we have discovered various techniques, mediums, and styles. We have admired renowned artists and celebrated their contributions. Yet, there remains an unspoken secret, a hidden gem in the world of art: face painting. In this chapter, we will shed light on the overlooked potential of face painting as a means to express creativity and earn a living. We will discuss why traditional high school art classes often fail to introduce students to this exciting art form and how you can tap into this market.

The Neglected Art: High school art classes, while valuable for building foundational skills, often focus on traditional mediums like painting, drawing, and sculpture. While these are essential, the curriculum typically disregards the vibrant art of face painting. This omission stems from various factors, including the historical emphasis on fine art and the lack of awareness about the potential within face painting.

I never understood why I was only taught about mainly 6 artist such as: Picasso, Andy Warhol, Van Gogh, Michelangelo, Donatello, and Leonardo. Yes, the Teenage Mutant Ninja Turtles. I honestly can't recall being taught about any black artist in school. As I continued to research and study while practicing self-education, I realized that I have never seen a black male face painter.

This is one reason why I believe that I could be a great and effective art teacher. I have experienced being selected to present my artwork in galleries. I have gained the know-it-all to start and maintain a lucrative face painting business, and I have learned how to use the art skills and transition to murals and residential painting. These things weren't taught to me in school. Face painting is a business that is seriously slept on.

The things that were taught to me in school to become successful, was to go to college and get degrees to go and work for a creditable company with hopes of being offered a promotion, and then retire after giving them thirty or forty years of your life. With face painting, there is no salary cap and you make your own rules. But, as with any freelancing position, you have to apply yourself and take advantage of every opportunity.

One should never attend any event with hundreds or thousands of people and not take the advantage of the crowd and advertise. Wear a shirt with your logo or pass out cards. Nowadays, your card should have a QR code printed on it so that one can scan and dispose of the card. To be honest, no one will want to keep your card. You want to try to gain followers because they can eventually turn into supporters.

With the inflation and recession at this day and time, I wouldn't recommend leaving your job and face painting full time. You will have to really stay on apps and in social media party groups to stay afloat. You MUST have competitive prices and quality work that equal or better than the competition. It is possible, but you have to take into consideration the status and income stability of potential clients. Personally, I stay at my job mainly for the benefits for my family but the consistent income is helpful as well.

The Cultural Shift: In recent years, there has been a noticeable shift in the perception of face painting. What was once seen as a mere novelty at carnivals and birthday parties has now evolved into a respected art form. Face painting has become a way to transform faces into living canvases, allowing artists to explore imaginative designs, intricate details, and storytelling through their creations. The demand for skilled face painters has skyrocketed, with opportunities ranging from corporate events and music festivals to theatrical productions and private parties.

Unlocking Creativity: Face painting opens up a whole new realm of creative possibilities. As an artist, you have the chance to blend colors, shapes, and patterns in ways that interact with the human face, utilizing its contours and expressions as an additional canvas. The dynamic nature of face painting allows you to experiment, adapt, and create unique designs that evoke emotions and captivate audiences. Unlike static art forms, face painting brings your art to life, enabling you to engage with people in a profoundly personal and interactive way.

Building a Business: One of the most remarkable aspects of face painting is its potential for financial success. While traditional art forms may present challenges in monetizing your skills, face painting offers numerous opportunities to earn a living as an artist. As the demand for face painters continues to rise, skilled practitioners can command competitive rates for their services. By establishing a strong portfolio, networking with event planners and entertainers, and actively marketing your services, you can build a thriving face painting business that provides both creative fulfillment and financial stability.

Embracing Face Painting: To embark on your face painting journey, you'll need to expand your artistic toolkit. Familiarize yourself with different types of face paints, brushes, sponges, and stencils. Learn techniques for creating various effects, such as blending, shading, and highlighting, specific to face painting. Practice on friends and family, experimenting with designs and refining your skills.

Additionally, seek out face painting workshops, online tutorials, and local art communities dedicated to this craft. Connect with experienced face painters who can provide guidance, mentorship, and insights into the industry. By immersing yourself in this vibrant community, you'll continue to grow as an artist and gain exposure to new opportunities.

Conclusion: While high school art classes may have overlooked the potential of face painting as a viable career path, it is never too late to embrace this captivating art form. By recognizing the artistry and business potential within face painting, you can unlock new avenues for creative expression and financial success. So, take a leap of faith, grab your brushes, and let the magic unfold as you explore the world of face painting.

CHAPTER 3:
UNLEASHING CREATIVITY
AND FLEXIBILITY

In the aftermath of a global recession and the unprecedented world-wide shutdown in the wake of the COVID-19 pandemic, the world had to redefine the way we work and generate income. Many industries were severely impacted, leaving individuals and families grappling with financial uncertainties. In these challenging times, some resilient individuals discovered the immense potential of servicing parties and exploring face painting as a second stream of income. What initially began as a necessity quickly evolved into a creative outlet that transformed lives and communities.

1. *Adapting to the New Normal:* In the wake of a recession, people were forced to reimagine their professional lives. Traditional job opportunities were scarce, and economic recovery was a slow and uncertain process. However, adversity often breeds innovation. People realized the need to adapt and explore alternative income sources. Servicing parties and face painting emerged as an unexpected solution that allowed individuals to harness their creativity, connect with others, and build a sustainable livelihood.

2. *The Power of Celebration:* During difficult times, the human spirit seeks solace and respite through celebration. Birthdays, anniversaries, and other joyous occasions became more significant than ever before. As people yearned to come together and commemorate special moments, the demand for party services skyrocketed. Entrepreneurs with an eye for opportunity recognized this trend and ventured into the party servicing industry, offering tailored solutions to suit various needs and budgets.

3. *Unleashing Creativity:* In a world stifled by uncertainty, party servicing became a canvas for creative expression. Individuals discovered that hosting and organizing events could be a platform to unleash their unique talents. From conceptualizing themes to designing captivating decorations, servicing parties provided an outlet for imaginative minds to flourish. This newfound creativity not only captivated audiences but also offered a sense of personal fulfillment and purpose.

4. *Face Painting:* The Art of Joy: One of the most enchanting aspects of party servicing was the introduction of face painting. A simple yet transformative art form, face painting captivated both children and adults alike. Skilled artists brought to life a vibrant array of characters, creatures, and designs on the canvas of smiling faces. The ability to create joy and wonder through a few brushstrokes became a cherished skill, providing artists with an additional source of income that was in high demand at events.

5. *Connecting Communities:* Beyond the financial benefits, servicing parties and face painting became catalysts for connection and community-building. As the world healed from the wounds of recession and isolation, these ventures breathed life into neighborhoods and brought people together. Through their services, entrepreneurs fostered a sense of unity and belonging. They became the threads that wove the fabric of society, creating lasting memories and forging meaningful relationships.

6. *Embracing the Second Stream of Income:* The experiences of those who ventured into servicing parties and face painting revealed the importance of diversifying income streams. In a world of uncertainty, relying on a single source of income can leave individuals vulnerable to economic downturns. These ventures allowed individuals to embrace the idea of multiple streams of income, giving them financial stability and the ability to weather future storms. I tell people that with parties, you can easily make an additional $100 an hour minimum.

Conclusion: The recession and the worldwide shutdown due to the COVID-19 pandemic brought about immense challenges, but they also fueled the spirit of resilience and innovation. Servicing parties and face painting emerged as not only a necessity but also a gateway to creativity, connection, and financial stability. The entrepreneurs who embraced these ventures not only found new ways to earn a living but also discovered the power of celebrating life, unleashing their creativity, and building communities. As we move forward, it is crucial to remember the lessons learned during these trying times and continue to seek opportunities that allow us to adapt, grow, and thrive.

CHAPTER 4:
BEING COMFORTABLE

As a black male face painter, I've attended many parties and events where I am one of the only people of color in attendance. I have never felt out of place or had any negative energy come towards my way. I know that my job is to entertain the kids. The adults have the freedom and right to engage with each other however they see fit.

I have serviced many parties in various locations, and sometimes, those parties involve substances like marijuana and alcohol. At first, these situations made me feel uncomfortable, but over time, I learned to navigate these environments and be comfortable in my own skin. You can feel uncomfortable because you are around strangers and you never know when a person has had more than they can handle. I have also experienced these things with different cultures.

One of the biggest challenges I faced early on was attending client's parties where I would be the only black person. These events were often filled with people who didn't look like me, and I sometimes felt out of place. But, as a face painter, I had a unique opportunity to break down barriers and connect with people through my art.

I quickly realized that my presence at these events was important, not just as a face painter, but as a black man. I could be a positive representation of my community and show people that we are more alike than different. So, I started to embrace these opportunities and found that people were genuinely interested in learning more about me and my work.

Of course, attending parties where marijuana and alcohol were present presented its own set of challenges. As a non-smoker and occasional drinker, I was concerned about being around substances that I wasn't comfortable with. But, again, I found that my role as a face painter gave me a unique perspective on these situations.

I learned that people who were using these substances were often more open and relaxed, which made it easier for me to connect with them. And, by being honest about my own boundaries and limitations, I found that people respected me more and were willing to accommodate my needs. By needs, I don't mean marijuana and alcohol.

I would never take a drink or beer while my face painting equipment is set up. If I am invited to the festivities, I always make sure that the job is complete and that I am paid in full. I don't want to have any photos or videos of me or my brand with alcohol over the internet. Then, I would be known as the drunk face painter and possibly become a meme.

I remember one Halloween weekend, I had four events in one day. At the third event, they were smoking and drinking. The host asked me did I want a drink. I kindly told her no because I had an event afterwards. I was worried that I could possibly smell like marijuana smoke heading to the next event. This made me adjust and start to carry an extra shirt to change in.

I ended up being 30 minutes late to my last event due to traffic. I stayed in constant communication with the client and discounted her for my tardiness. If I would've taken the drink and arrived smelling like marijuana, that would make her never want to work with me again. What surprised me when I arrived, was a lady attending the party spoke to me by first name. She said that they had visited my Facebook page days prior to the event. Keep your social media clean, because people will review your post history and research you. Once set up, I took care of business and she offered me a twenty dollar tip when I was done. I told her that I couldn't accept it due to my tardiness.

Last but not least, going to locations that I am unfamiliar with can sometimes be a little uncomfortable. I never know what type of area or what type of police that they may have. Some may think that I am over thinking or a little paranoid. I say that you are right. Seeing the killings of unarmed black men on the news and social media does have somewhat of a slight effect on my mental calmness.

In many ways, being a black male face painter has taught me to be comfortable in uncomfortable situations. It has given me a platform to connect with people who are different from me and to break down stereotypes and barriers. And, it has shown me that, with an open mind and an open heart, anything is possible.

CHAPTER 5:
PLEASE, DON'T LEAN ON MY TABLE

Face painting is a fun activity for kids, and it's always a hit at parties and events. However, when you're the face painter, it's essential to set some ground rules for the children waiting in line. Kids are full of energy and excitement, and it can be challenging to keep them from getting out of control. Here are some rules that you can set to make sure that the face painting experience goes smoothly for everyone involved.

All of the kids are excited and you will meet different personalities. Some kids will be calm and patient and some kids will walk out of line and come to see what you are painting. For example, some kids will lean in front of you while you are painting to see what you are putting on the next child's face. They will literally block your vision with their head. Really?

Setting rules for kids in the face painting line is a must when the adults are not helping keep organization and order. Some parents look at you as the babysitter while they provide hospitality. You are hired to face paint, not babysit. At times, you will be the only hired entertainment. It is understandable at parties that the kids will flock to you and surround you with energy and happiness. Remind them that everyone is going to get their faces painted so this calms done the aggression and impatient energy.

Rule #1: Don't Lean on the Table
When kids are waiting in line for face painting, they may be tempted to lean on the table. However, leaning on the table can cause the paint and brushes to move around, which can lead to spills or accidents. The movement and weight can also knock over your table. To prevent this from happening, make sure that you tell the kids not to lean on the table. You can also put up a sign that reminds them of this rule.

Rule #2: Don't Sit Your Cups on the Table

When kids are waiting in line, they may also want to put their cups or other items on the table. However, this can cause spills or other accidents. To prevent this from happening, make sure that you tell the kids not to put their cups on the table. You can also provide a separate area where they can put their cups or other items. They will also place party bags, cotton candy, trash, glasses, hair ties, and whatever they may have on your table. Keep a close watch, because you will be finished painting with 4 water bottles on your table and no one in your chair.

Rule #3: Don't Touch the Paint or Brushes

Some kids may be tempted to touch the paint or brushes while they're waiting in line. However, this can cause the paint to get smudged or contaminated, which can ruin the face painting experience for everyone. To prevent this from happening, make sure that you tell the kids not to touch the paint or brushes. You can also keep the paint and brushes out of reach.

Younger kids will see the paint brushes and think that it is coloring time. I have went to the restroom and come back to find a toddler mixing the colors with a brush in their hand. Toddlers are difficult to be seen standing behind a table with a cover over it.

Rule #4: Stay in Line

When kids are waiting in line for face painting, it's essential that they stay in line. Moving around or cutting in line can cause confusion and disrupt the process. To prevent this from happening, make sure that you tell the kids to stay in line and wait their turn. You can also have a staff member or volunteer monitor the line to ensure that everyone stays in order.

Many times you will have a kid that has been waiting, leave the line and go to play or do other things and then come back and try to be the next person to get in the chair. As the face painter, you can't watch the line and paint at the same time. Sometimes you can remember the line order but most often at times you can't. In this type of situation, I just tell the kid that they have to stay in line in order to be painted.

Rule #5: Be Patient

Face painting can take time, especially if there are a lot of kids waiting in line. To prevent kids from getting restless or bored, make sure that you encourage them to be patient. You can also provide activities or games to keep them occupied while they wait.

I personally like to play music. My favorite song to play and watch the kids sing and dance is the song from the movie, "Madagascar – I Like to Move It". This gets all of the kids and parents moving and singing. This is one way that I stand out versus other face painters.

Setting rules for kids in a face painting line is essential to ensure that everyone has a safe and enjoyable experience. By following these rules, you can help prevent accidents and keep the line moving smoothly. Remember to communicate the rules clearly and enforce them consistently to ensure that everyone has a fun and memorable time.

At times, you can hear kids say things like, it's taking so long, or I wish he would hurry up. I simply reply, "Well, I will paint fast when I get to you". This usually hushes the kid up respectfully.

CHAPTER 6:
PAINTING SMILES ON DIFFERENT FACES

As a face painter, I've had the privilege of meeting children from different backgrounds and income levels. While each child is unique, their reactions to getting their face painted are often similar. Seeing their faces light up with excitement and wonder is one of the most rewarding experiences I've ever had.

One of the most memorable events I've participated in was a church carnival in a Richardson, Texas neighborhood. This event was well organized. A day before the event, they sent me a map of the setup, parking, and all instructions and rules needed for the day of the event. The kids were so excited to see all the activities and treats, and the face painting booth was no exception. I was in a room with 3 other face painters. Many of the children had never had their faces painted before, and they were so eager to choose their designs.

The church designated an hour and a half for all special needs children. This was a heartwarming moment for me. Seeing the smiles on those faces almost made me shed a tear. I remember one little boy who was very shy and hesitant to approach the booth at first, but once he saw the other children getting painted, he finally decided to try it. This usually happens with kids. He chose a Spiderman design and was so thrilled with the result that he couldn't stop smiling.

Also, this event had over 25,000 people confirming that they were going. It was a cold day, so that 25,000 ended up being a little over 10,000. I was glad that we were setup indoors. I had never been or seen an event like this in my life. We worked for 5 hours and I was paid $100 per hour. I also gained some new customers from painting that day.

Recently, someone called the church looking for me to paint at a kid's party. When we finally got in contact with one another, I was already booked for that time slot. That person was disappointed. This shows that you never know who is watching and when an opportunity to paint will present itself.

When dealing with special needs children, patience is a necessity. You will experience a lot of flinching, head turning, and just complete movement. The parents usually will tell you of any actions that may cause them behave in a certain way. One could be nonverbal or one may not like to be able to remove their glasses and so on. Be versatile and able to adapt to give the kid a memorable face painting experience. I aim to create memories and allow clients to cherish the moments while having fun doing it.

Another event that stands out in my mind was the NFL Buffalo Bill's linebacker, Von Miller Day in Desoto, Texas. I made the mistake of bringing my Seattle Seahawks tent to the giveback celebration. Von has only played for the Denver Broncos, Los Angeles Rams, and Buffalo Bills. He funded the entire festival. I don't know what I was thinking, but it was the only tent that I had. I was asked to take it down by one of the coordinators of the event. I understood their perspective and immediately packed it away.

In addition, once I was set up and prepared to paint, a big gust of wind came and blew over my table and face painting case. I had cards, glitter, paint brushes, and face paint rolling and flying everywhere. Luckily, I had a great group of people at the event. Around five people rushed over to help me pick up everything. I didn't stress or neither was I embarrassed. I live life as, take it how it comes and go with the flow. This means that you have to be versatile and be able to adapt in any situation. Getting angry wouldn't have been like a Thanos snap, and rewind time. I just took a deep breath and prepared my mind for what could have been a difficult day, but it wasn't.

Towards the last hour at the end of an event, I usually estimate how long it would take me to finish the line and deny any new customers. At events most of the time, people fail to listen. Parents were still lining up to get their kids face painted. I had to learn to say no. When I didn't get booked as much, I would stay and paint everyone to continue to gain practice and create muscle memory. I had a party to service right after the Von Miller event. I had to pack up and leave. This mostly happens when you are painting at a free event.

Parents were saying things like, we have been waiting in line or can she just get a heart. Although, I know that it would mean the world to the kid, I also know that if I do one, the others would want the same. I try to break it to them easily as I can. "I have a party that has already paid me to be there at this time. If I didn't have another engagement, then I would happily paint your child. I hope you can understand. Here's my card in case you ever need a face painter for an event."

I let them know that it is nothing personal, but it's business. Even though they may have arrived late, if I was able to paint them, I would. If you go to a restaurant to get chicken and they tell you that they will possibly run out of chicken, do you stay in line if there is no guarantee that you will get your chicken or try again at another time.

CHAPTER 7:
EVENTS

At events, you will see kids from all demographics. You will have hourly paid events and events that you can charge per child. To not overwork yourself at hourly paid events, choose small designs or use a stencil. People will come and expect the most because it is free for them. A lot of times they will not tip either, so instead of having 20 kids in 2 hours like at a birthday party, you will have 40 or 50 in a line waiting, expecting paying client services.

At a paying customer event, this is when you showcase your skills. Take a little more time on your clients. You will have both young and old clients. Paint every face like you want them to advertise for you. Be sure to give your contact information to each customer because it could lead to future jobs or gigs. Choose a price range that is affordable but also is profitable for you in the end.

A lot of times, if you are working an event and you are a vendor, you will have to pay to attend. Take into consideration the weather, location, time, and the type of other vendors that are attending. This is crucial because it allows you to predetermine if the other vendors would draw the type of crowd that you need.

For example, I wouldn't want to be a face painter at an event catering to mainly adults. If I were to partake, I would try to sell my art or art prints. If the event was having popcorn, bounce houses, cotton candy, and more than I would most definitely attend depending on the price.

Speaking of price, it will vary depending on the type of venue and the locations. Be prepared to pay anywhere from $25 to $150. If you are paying on the high end, then there should be thousands of people in attendance. This price should only be closer to the holidays. The low end would be your random weekend or weekday events.

Some event planners or coordinators will want you to be setup an hour before the event starts. This gives you time to setup and prepare your mind for what's to come. If you are running late, because things happen, then it is a possibility that you will still be on time if your target arrival time is the earliest time given.

What I learned at events were to invest in a wagon. I had to make 3 and 4 trips back and forward to the car just to load and unload. Through observation, I saw other people using table covers, wagons, signs or banners, table tops and more. The one thing that stood out to me was that everyone was using black table covers. I decided to use a neon color so that in the future, I would pop out when potential customers walk into the room. I also found that a wagon makes it much easier to transport your equipment. I would highly recommend it.

When kids come to my booth they let loose and show their true excitement. They are thrilled to get their faces painted, as all children. It reminds me that no matter what's their background, children just want to have fun and be themselves.

I've also painted faces at festivals and events that catered to a wide range of ages and interests. At these events, I've painted faces of children who were fans of superheroes, animals, flowers, and even abstract designs. One of my favorite designs to paint for little girls is the unicorn design with glitter. My favorite design for boys would be the unknown, because whenever I think that I have done my research and I'm prepared for what's to come, the kids always ask for something that I have never painted before.

What I've learned from these experiences is that children are more alike than they are different. No matter their background or income level, they all share a desire for fun and playfulness. As a face painter, I have the privilege of bringing that joy to their faces and helping them forget about their worries for a little while. It's a reminder that we can all benefit from a little bit of childlike wonder and playfulness in our lives.

My first year of painting, I didn't understand that you have to select colors based on skin color or the shades of the skin. I had a little girl that came and asked for a Hello Kitty face but with orange paint. I didn't consider that her having darker skin would not allow the paint to be visible on her face, and then I outlined it in black.

She went inside and came out about a minute later stating that her brother said to paint her face again. Being new to face painting, I replied with, "Tell your brother that I'm not painting anything again." She went and told her brother. He came outside with his pants sagging and his head tilted speaking with a slur, "You painted my sister face"?

I am naturally sarcastic, so as I looked around in every direction, I replied, "I'm the only person out here painting faces". Then his mother came outside and said leave that man alone. Remember I told you how I grew up in my first book, "You're the Face Painter". Also, these were not paying customers. Kids will request a face painting and an arm painting. Some parents will stand there as if they've hired you and think that they're kid is required to get what they requested, even with 15 people in line behind them.

I was in Plano, Texas painting for a community block party. They had fireman and policeman in attendance. I painted for 2 hours, but as I was leaving a band was setting up and caterers were bringing in food. I was feeling like I'm about to miss the party. I also seen this time as an opportunity to interact with law enforcement.

I asked one of the police officers to do a skit. I wanted him to act as if he arrested me for impersonating a face painter. I was trying to go viral because this was not to long after the world opened back up from covid. He told me that they wasn't allowed to do so and by me being of a different culture, it could possibly cause riots and much more, because I am a black male face painter and he is a white police officer. I told him that I understood his position and walk to take a photo with the firemen.

CHAPTER 8:
CONVERSATION WHILE PAINTING

Kids say the darnest things. They speak the truth, they have impulsive reactions, and they are direct with their message. The delivery of the message will differ depending on the demographics. In one location, the kid may say, "Oooh, your breath stank", and in another location, a child may say, "your breath smells really bad". Although, I have never heard these things, I keep a mint and dental hygiene in the car.

As a black male face painter, I always felt like an outsider in the world of children's entertainment. But I soon discovered that being different was my greatest strength. Kids were fascinated by me because I looked like them, and yet other's because I was unlike any other face painter they had ever seen.

At first, I struggled to find work as a face painter. I would show up to events, only to be turned away because organizers assumed he was there to cause trouble or that kids wouldn't want a black male face painter. As soon as I started painting, the kids were mesmerized. They loved watching iPAINT turn their faces into lions, tigers, and superheroes. They asked me questions about my life and my art, and I was happy to answer them.

Over time, I became a regular at local events, and my reputation grew. Parents appreciated my unique perspective and the way I connect with their kids. I never talked down to the kids, and I always listened to what they had to say. I aim to become a role model for many young black boys who rarely see men who look like them in the world of children's entertainment.

But iPAINT didn't just connect with black kids. I had a gift for putting all kids at ease, no matter their race or background. I make them feel special by creating one-of-a-kind designs on their faces, and I always have a smile and a kind word for everyone.

Through face painting, I found my calling. I realize that my art could bring people together and bridge gaps between different communities. I will continue to paint faces and inspire children for years to come, and will always be grateful for the chance to make a difference in their lives.

One experience that I had was a kid getting in my chair and I asked him his age, grade, and what did he want on his face. He told me what he wanted, and as I was painting he said, "I'm surprised that my dad's not drunk yet." I was speechless at first but then I tried to change the conversation and ask has he seen the latest movie that had been released. Expect the unexpected when dealing with kids.

I was in Josephine, Texas and there were a group of teenagers at a party. They were enjoying life, you know like teens do. They were giggling, talking, and pushing each other and just being teens. One teen got in the chair and said that his friends were going to choose his face art. His friend leaned towards me and asks me to paint a cock on his face. I told him that I wouldn't do it and that it would not be good for me and my business. These was a group of white teens and if I had painted what he ask, I probably wouldn't have had a job in that area again.

CHAPTER 9:
WEATHERPROOF

Face painting is a fantastic art form that is loved by people of all ages. One of the great things about face painting is its versatility, which allows it to be done indoors in any weather and outdoors in appropriate weather conditions. In this chapter, we will explore how face painting is weatherproof and discuss the benefits of being able to paint faces in any climate.

When it comes to face painting, weather can be a concern. If it's raining or too hot outside, it can be difficult to do face painting comfortably. However, with the proper planning and preparation, face painting can be done in any weather. For indoor events, there's no need to worry about weather conditions. You can paint faces in the comfort of your own home, in a studio, or at a party venue without being affected by the weather.

In contrast, when it comes to outdoor events, it's important to be mindful of the weather conditions. While face painting can be done outdoors in appropriate weather, it's crucial to take precautions to protect both the artist and the participants. For example, on a hot day, it's important to make sure that the artist is in a shaded area to avoid heat exhaustion. Additionally, participants should be encouraged to drink plenty of water to stay hydrated.

On the other hand, in cooler weather conditions, the artist should ensure that their equipment is not affected by the weather. For example, water-based face paint may freeze if the temperature is too cold. Therefore, the artist may need to use a different type of paint or make sure the paint is kept warm to avoid freezing.

Some customers insist on keeping the party outdoors even when the weather doesn't permit. It's uncomfortable for the kid because the water makes the face paint cold and the face painter, because our hands are cold. This makes it harder to paint straight lines and just kind of makes us rush the job.

One of the benefits of face painting being weatherproof is that it allows for more opportunities to showcase the art form. For example, if an outdoor event is planned, the face painter can be a valuable addition to the event by providing entertainment that is weather-resistant. In addition, indoor events can benefit from the versatility of face painting by being able to host events in any weather condition.

In conclusion, face painting is a weatherproof art form that can be enjoyed both indoors and outdoors. While it's important to take precautions when painting faces in different weather conditions, the versatility of face painting allows for more opportunities to showcase the art form. Whether it's raining or sunny outside, face painting is an activity that can be enjoyed in any weather condition, making it a fantastic addition to any event. In Texas heat, I get happy when the party is indoors.

CHAPTER 10:
FACE PAINTING VS. BOUNCE HOUSES

When it comes to entertaining children, two popular options are face painting and bounce houses. Both activities are great ways to keep kids engaged and having fun, but which one is better? In this chapter, we'll explore the pros and cons of face painting and bounce houses to help you decide which option is best for your event.

Pros of Face Painting:

1. Creativity: Face painting offers endless possibilities for creativity. Children can choose from a variety of designs and colors to create a look that is uniquely theirs. It's a great way to encourage self-expression and imagination.

2. Interactive: Face painting is a one-on-one experience that allows for personal interaction between the child and the artist. It's a great opportunity to make a connection and bond with each child, creating a positive and memorable experience.

3. Safe: When done properly, face painting is a safe activity for children. High-quality, non-toxic paints and proper hygiene practices can ensure that there is no risk of allergic reactions or skin irritation.

Cons of Face Painting:

1. Time-Consuming: Face painting can be a time-consuming activity, especially if there are a lot of children to paint. Each design can take several minutes to complete, which can slow down the flow of your event.

2. Limited Availability: Face painters can be difficult to find and book, especially during peak event seasons. If you're planning an

event last minute, it may be challenging to secure a face painter worth your money.

3. Weather-Dependent: Face painting is an indoor or outdoor activity, depending on the weather. If you're planning an event outdoors and it starts to rain, you may need to cancel the face painting portion of your event.

Pros of Bounce Houses:

1. Fun: Bounce houses are a lot of fun for children. They can jump and play for hours, burning off energy and staying entertained.

2. Inclusive: Bounce houses can accommodate a large number of children at once, making them an inclusive activity for groups. Children of all ages and abilities can participate.

3. Easy Setup: Bounce houses are relatively easy to set up and take down. They can be rented from party supply companies and come with all the necessary equipment.

Cons of Bounce Houses:

1. Safety Concerns: Bounce houses can pose safety risks if not set up and supervised properly. Children can get hurt if they fall or collide with each other inside the bounce house.

2. Limited Creativity: Bounce houses offer limited opportunities for creativity. Children can jump and play, but they cannot express themselves in the same way as they can with face painting.

3. Weather-Dependent: Like face painting, bounce houses are weather-dependent. If it's too hot, cold, or raining, you may need to cancel the bounce house portion of your event.

Conclusion:

Both face painting and bounce houses have their pros and cons. Face painting offers a creative and interactive experience, but can be time-consuming and limited in availability. Bounce houses provide a fun and inclusive activity, but can be dangerous if not set up and super-vised properly. Ultimately, the choice between face painting and bounce houses depends on your event's specific needs and goals. If you want to encourage creativity and personal interaction, face painting may be the way to go. If you're looking for a fun and inclusive activity that accommodates a large number of children, a bounce house may be the better option.

CHAPTER 11:
NO MORE CLOWNS

When it comes to face painting, many people often associate the activity with clowns. However, dressing up as a clown isn't always necessary to have fun with face paint. In fact, one can even wear a simple t-shirt to elevate their face painting game.

The concept of wearing a t-shirt instead of a full clown costume is not a new idea. It's a trend that has been gaining popularity in recent years, especially among those who prefer a more minimalist approach to face painting. Not only is it more comfortable, but it also allows for more creativity in design and expression.

One of the main advantages of wearing a t-shirt is that it provides a blank canvas for the face paint. It allows the design to take center stage, without any distracting clothing or accessories. A simple white or black t-shirt is perfect for this purpose, but any color or pattern can work depending on the design.

Another advantage of wearing a t-shirt is the convenience factor. A clown costume can be bulky and difficult to move around in, making it challenging to interact with children or entertain a crowd. Wearing a t-shirt, on the other hand, allows for a full range of movement and makes it easier to engage with the audience.

Also, if you can recall, there were multiple videos of clowns chasing and attacking strangers on social media. This does not help with advertisement to kids when they see those clowns, and the clown from the movie "It". Also, as a black male, I don't feel comfortable riding in my car with a painted face going to certain locations in my state.

Of course, there are some downsides to wearing a t-shirt instead of a full clown costume. It may not have the same impact or level of recognition as a clown outfit, which may be important for those who want to establish a brand or reputation as a clown. Additionally, some may argue that a clown costume adds to the overall experience and atmosphere of the event.

However, for those who are simply looking to have fun with face paint and entertain children, wearing a t-shirt can be a great alternative. It allows for more creative expression, is more comfortable, and is more convenient for interacting with the audience.

In conclusion, while dressing up as a clown for face painting is a classic option, it's not the only way to enjoy the activity. Wearing a t-shirt provides a simple and effective alternative that allows for more creativity, comfort, and convenience. Give it a try and see how it can enhance your face painting experience.

If you have a logo, I recommend that you wear a shirt with you logo and social media information. It helps make your logo recognizable to the eye and sometimes people may want to know if you have merchandise for sale. This will create additional income.

CHAPTER 12:
DEMANDING CUSTOMERS

As a black male face painter, you are no stranger to difficult customers. While most people are happy with the results of your work, there are always those few who seem impossible to please. But don't worry, with a little bit of patience and some effective communication skills, you can successfully deal with even the most demanding customers.

The first step in dealing with demanding customers is to understand their expectations. Take the time to listen carefully to what they want and try to get a sense of their vision. Once you understand their expectations, you can work to manage them. Be honest with the customer about what you can and cannot do. If they have unrealistic expectations, gently explain the limitations of face painting and offer alternatives.

Another important tip for dealing with demanding customers is to stay calm and professional. It can be easy to get frustrated when someone is being difficult, but it's important to keep your cool. Remember, you are a professional and your reputation is on the line. Take a deep breath, smile, and maintain a positive attitude.

Communication is key when dealing with demanding customers. Make sure you are clear and concise when explaining your process and what the customer can expect. It's also important to set boundaries and stick to them. If the customer is requesting something outside of your scope, politely let them know that it is not possible.

In some cases, it may be necessary to compromise with the customer. If the request is reasonable and within your capabilities, try to find a middle ground that will satisfy both parties. However, if their request is simply not possible, be firm but polite in your response.

Demanding and difficult are two separate experiences. I recently had a customer reach out to me on an app about a gig. I stated that my pictures don't load on the app sometimes and that I would send him pics to his phone. When I sent the pictures, he replied, "don't ever send pics in bulk like that... what a terrible unprofessional thing to do. Goodbye." This method has worked for me dozens of times. I replied and told him that this experience would be going in my book, and then I blocked his number. You can choose who you want to work with when selecting jobs. If the energy is not positive, I would pass on the opportunity.

Finally, it's important to remember that not every customer will be happy, no matter how hard you try. If you've done everything in your power to meet their expectations and they are still unhappy, don't take it personally. Some people are simply impossible to please. Instead, focus on the positive feedback you receive from the vast majority of your customers.

Dealing with demanding customers can be challenging, but with the right mindset and communication skills, you can successfully manage their expectations and provide excellent service. Remember, you are a professional face painter and your skills and expertise are valuable. Don't let difficult customers undermine your confidence and always strive to provide the best possible experience for your clients.

CHAPTER 13:
PAINTING ALL AGES

As a black male face painter, I've had the opportunity to work with clients of all ages, races, and backgrounds. One of the things I love most about my job is the diverse range of people I get to meet and work with. Over the years, I've had the pleasure of painting the faces of some of the oldest and youngest clients I've ever had.

The oldest client I ever worked with was an 88-year-old woman. She was attending a Halloween party. She had moved to Texas with her daughter and son-in-law from California. I was the first face painter to paint them in Texas. They are now returning customers, and have invited me and my family to attend the next party. At first, I was a little apprehensive about painting the face of someone so advanced in age, but I soon realized that age was just a number. The woman was full of life and energy, and she was just as excited as any of any kid that I have ever painted.

As I started to paint her face, I couldn't help but feel a sense of joy and admiration for this woman. Despite her age, she was still curious and adventurous, willing to try something new and fun. When I finished painting her face, she looked in the mirror and smiled with delight. It was a beautiful moment, and it reminded me that you're never too old to enjoy the simple pleasures in life.

On the other end of the spectrum, I also had the pleasure of painting the face of an 8-month-old baby. The baby's grandmother brought him to a local fair, and they wanted to get his face painted to commemorate the occasion. Painting the face of a baby was a completely different experience from painting the face of an adult. Babies are naturally curious and wiggly, and they don't always stay still for very long. But with patience and a gentle touch, I was able to paint a cute little design on the baby's cheek.

The baby's father and grandmother were thrilled with the results, and they took lots of pictures to remember the moment. The grandmother was an old classmate of mine and just wanted to support me. It was heartwarming to see the joy on their faces as they watched their little one experience something new and exciting.

Working with clients of all ages is one of the things that makes being a face painter so rewarding. Whether I'm painting the face of an 88-year-old woman or an 8-month-old baby, each client brings their own unique energy and spirit to the experience. It's an honor to be able to create something that brings joy and happiness to people of all ages, and I feel grateful every day to be able to do what I love.

CHAPTER 14:
BEST CULTURES TO PAINT

There is really no difference painting at different cultured parties. Some families will offer you food, drink, and cake and some don't. I have experienced this with every culture. I can say that the older women at the parties will fix a plate for me to go. OMG, the older women fix some of the best plates. I usually eat while driving home or to my next gig.

Some people take me being comfortable into heavy consideration. I have no complaints about that. I have had someone turn the big fan cooling the venue of an event and aim it in my direction denying anyone else a breeze. I have had people bring me drinks and open it for me as I paint. Some families encourage me to take a break and eat. There are friendly people in the world, both male and female. They treat people with respect, spread love, and good positive energy and that's in all cultures.

I've worked at parties where the parents were laid back and let me be creative, and I've worked at parties where the parents were stricter and wanted traditional designs. But overall, I've found that there is a noticeable difference in the way that I approach face painting at different types of events.

As a black male face painter, it's important for me to be able to adapt to the needs and expectations of my clients, regardless of their cultural background. Whether I'm painting at a white, Asian, Indian, Mexican, or black party, my goal is always the same - to create beautiful and memorable designs that bring joy to the children and their families.

I couldn't help but feel a surge of offense when I noticed the teenage girl's father leaning in to whisper something in her ear just moments before I was about to begin painting her face. The whispers, accompanied by a subtle shift in their demeanor, sparked a sense of unease within me. The father's actions raised questions in my mind about their intentions and whether my gender was a factor in their interaction.

Being aware of the historical and ongoing challenges faced by male individuals, I couldn't help but wonder if their whispered conversation was fueled by prejudice or misguided assumptions. It reminded me of the countless instances where people have been subjected to unfair treatment based solely on the color of their skin or their gender. Though I remained professional and committed to delivering a delightful face painting experience, a seed of discomfort had been planted, highlighting the persistent need for awareness and progress in matters of equality. If I had been a female face painter, would he have done the same? This gentleman was a black man, and the event was at a church. From a father's perspective I could understand his discussion with his daughter, but from a face painter's perspective, it made me think to myself, is that what people think of me.

In Indian culture, it is not uncommon to find children who are captivated by the vibrant traditions and customs that surround them. However, to my surprise, the kids politely declined the offer of face painting. Instead, they expressed a keen desire to have their delicate hands painted. Eagerly extending their palms, these culturally conscious children sought to embrace a cherished aspect of their heritage.

I was at a party located in Dallas, Texas close to the Galleria Mall. I could see a Hispanic man watching me as I painted the kids. It seemed as if he would get closer and closer to me every time that I would look up. His chair would move a few inches after every kid. As I finished the last kid, he walked up to me and asked me was I done painting. I asked was he trying to get his face painted, and he said that he was. He told me that he had never had his face painted and that he just wanted to scrap it off of his bucket list. I painted a partial reptile print covering his cheek, eye, and half of his forehead. He smiled the rest of the day and gave me ten dollars. Every adult still has a piece of a kid inside of them.

CHAPTER 15:
FACE PAINTING FOR BIG NAME COMPANIES

Face painting in recent years has become a popular way for companies to connect with their customers in a fun and engaging way. As a black male face painter, I have had the privilege of working with some of the biggest household name companies in the world, and in this chapter, I will share my insights on what it takes to succeed in this field.

First and foremost, it is essential to have a strong portfolio. Companies want to see that you have experience in face painting, and that you can create high-quality designs that will appeal to their target audience. This means investing time in developing your skills, experimenting with different techniques, and building a diverse range of designs that can be tailored to specific events or campaigns.

When it comes to working with household name companies, it's important to understand their brand and messaging. Every company has a unique identity, and their face painting designs should reflect this. For example, if you are working with a toy company, your designs should be fun and playful, while if you are working with a sports team, your designs should be bold and eye-catching.

Communication is key when working with household name companies. You will need to be able to listen carefully to their needs and preferences, and be able to provide suggestions and feedback based on your experience. This means being comfortable with taking direction, but also being confident in your abilities and offering your own ideas and input.

One of the most important skills for a face painter working with household name companies is flexibility. You will need to be able to adapt to different environments and work with different types of people, from marketing executives to event coordinators to children and families. This means being able to work well under pressure, staying calm and focused in fast-paced environments, and being able to quickly adjust your designs based on the situation.

I have had the pleasure of face painting for Chicken N Pickle. I was hired to partake in their Easter event one year. As of now, this company has 7 locations in the USA, and 2 of the 7 are in Texas. There will be a third location in Allen, Texas soon. I painted at the Grand Prairie location. I had never been or heard of Chicken N Pickle until being hired for the position. I believe that I was hired through social media, Facebook to be exact.

When I arrived, I could see the Kermit green chairs and décor everywhere. I waited for my contact to meet me and escort me to my working location. They had a table set up for me and I didn't have to use the one that I was carrying. As soon as I was ready to paint, the line kept a minimum of 20 people. It moved pretty fast because most of the customers were asking for bunnies because it was an Easter event. I was grateful for the opportunity. My only regret is that I didn't get enough footage of the event. This was before social media reels and TikTok.

Next, I was hired to paint for Williams Chicken. Yes, another chicken spot. The founder had a community center named after him, Hiawatha Williams. The first location was opened in 1987 in Dallas, Texas. Today, there are over 40 locations in operation. The majority of the Williams Chicken stores are located in the Dallas/Fort Worth metro area. I didn't know what type of an event that I was working. That was a good learning opportunity for myself, ask better questions besides the location and timeframe.

The same day, I was scheduled by the same event coordinators to paint for a Chevrolet car dealership. It was cold and rainy, and the only space sufficient enough for the activities were outside the facility. When the wind would blow, you could feel mist of water fall on your skin. None of those things stopped people from standing in line to wait to get their faces painted. I tried to wear gloves to keep my hands warm while I painted but it affected the quality of the finished faces. After all, I still made the best of the circumstances and stayed professional.

I couldn't do this without the help of my supporters and social media followers. I am grateful for them, because anytime someone is searching for a face painter; they will tag me and recommend me. Some of them have positions and connections that their words have power and if they say it, then it is done. Once connected with these people, my genuine spirit and personality play a part in creating a bond.

Finally, professionalism is key. When working with household name companies, you are representing their brand, so it is important to be punctual, well-presented, and respectful at all times. You will need to be able to work well with others, including other face painters, event staff, and members of the public, and always maintain a positive and friendly attitude.

In conclusion, face painting for household name companies can be a rewarding and exciting career for black male face painters. By developing a strong portfolio, understanding the company's brand and messaging, communicating effectively, being flexible, and maintaining a professional demeanor, you can create high-quality designs that will help companies connect with their customers in a fun and engaging way.

CHAPTER 16:
TRANSITIONING FROM ARTIST TO FACE PAINTER

Introduction: Transitioning from being a traditional artist to a face painter can be an exciting and rewarding journey. The ability to transform a blank canvas into a living, breathing work of art on someone's face is a unique and captivating skill. In this chapter, we will explore the steps needed to successfully transition into the world of face painting.

Step 1: Expand Your Artistic Skillset As an artist; you already possess a strong foundation in creativity and visual expression. However, face painting requires additional skills and techniques. Start by researching and studying face painting tutorials, books, and online resources. Familiarize yourself with the different brushes, paints, and techniques commonly used in face painting. Practice on yourself, friends, or family members to develop your skills and gain confidence in handling the tools of the trade.

Step 2: Attend Workshops and Classes To accelerate your learning process and gain insights from experienced face painters, consider attending workshops and classes. Look for local art schools, community centers, or face painting conventions that offer courses specifically designed for aspiring face painters. These opportunities will provide you with hands-on experience, guidance, and feedback from professionals in the field. Embrace every chance to learn from others and absorb their knowledge.

Step 3: Research and Understand Safety Guidelines Face painting involves direct contact with a person's skin, so it is crucial to prioritize safety and hygiene. Research and familiarize yourself with the industry's safety guidelines, such as using FDA-compliant cosmetic-grade paints, cleaning brushes and tools thoroughly, and maintaining a sanitary work environment. Ensuring the well-being of your clients is of utmost importance and will establish your credibility as a professional face painter.

Step 4: Build a Portfolio As you refine your skills, start building a portfolio of your face painting work. Capture high-quality photographs of your designs to showcase your abilities. Include a diverse range of designs, such as animals, superheroes, fantasy characters, and abstract patterns. Consider creating a website or using social media platforms to display your portfolio. A strong online presence will help attract potential clients and serve as a platform to share your passion for face painting with the world.

Step 5: Network and Collaborate to establish yourself as a face painter, it is essential to network and collaborate with others in the industry. Connect with local event planners, party organizers, and entertainers who may require your services. Attend community events, fairs, and festivals to showcase your work and make connections. Collaborating with other artists or face painters on joint projects can also help expand your reach and inspire new ideas.

Step 6: Market Yourself Promote your face painting services through various marketing channels. Create business cards, flyers, or brochures that highlight your unique style and contact information. Leverage social media platforms by sharing your work, engaging with followers, and offering special promotions. Consider partnering with local businesses that cater to children, such as toy stores or party supply shops, to cross-promote your services.

Step 7: Constantly Learn and Evolve The world of face painting is continuously evolving, and it is important to stay updated with the latest trends, techniques, and tools. Attend industry conferences, join online communities, and follow renowned face painters to stay connected and learn from their experiences.

Experiment with new styles and challenge yourself to push the boundaries of your creativity.

Conclusion: Transitioning from being a traditional artist to a face painter requires dedication, practice, and a willingness to learn. By expanding your skillset, attending workshops, adhering to safety guidelines, building a strong portfolio, networking, marketing yourself, and staying current with industry trends, you can successfully make the leap into the world of face painting. Embrace the journey, let your creativity flourish, and watch

CHAPTER 17:
BALLOON TWISTING
VS. FACE PAINTING:
A BATTLE OF CREATIVITY

Introduction:

In the colorful realm of children's entertainment, two artistic mediums have captured the imaginations of both kids and adults alike: balloon twisting and face painting. Both of these crafts possess the power to transform ordinary moments into extraordinary experiences, sprinkling joy and wonder into the lives of young ones. In this chapter, we will discuss the pros and cons of balloon twisting and face painting, exploring the unique attributes and considerations that accompany each art form.

Section 1: The Art of Balloon Twisting

Pros of Balloon Twisting:

1. Instant Gratification: Balloon twisting offers immediate satisfaction, as the sculpting process unfolds before the eyes of the children. With a few quick twists and turns, an ordinary balloon can be transformed into a whimsical creature, captivating young imaginations and creating memorable moments.

2. Interactive and Engaging: Balloon twisting involves direct interaction between the entertainer and the children. As the artist skillfully crafts various shapes and animals, children can participate, offering suggestions and witnessing their ideas come to life. This interactive element fosters engagement, encouraging children to feel like part of the creative process.

3. Versatility and Variety: Balloons come in a vast array of colors and sizes, offering endless possibilities for creativity. From

classic animals like dogs and rabbits to fantastical creatures like unicorns and dragons, balloon twisting allows entertainers to explore different themes and designs, adapting to any event or preference.

Cons of Balloon Twisting:

1. Limited Longevity: Despite the visual appeal and instant gratification, balloon sculptures are temporary creations. Over time, balloons gradually deflate, losing their charm and shape. This limited lifespan can be disappointing for children who wish to hold onto their balloon animals for an extended period.

2. Fragility and Safety Concerns: While balloons are generally safe, they can pop or burst unexpectedly, causing potential safety hazards. Young children, in their excitement, may mishandle or accidentally ingest small balloon pieces. Balloon twisters must exercise caution and closely supervise the use of balloons to prevent any mishaps.

Section 2: The Craft of Face Painting

Pros of Face Painting:

1. Personalized Expression: Face painting provides a canvas on which children can express their individuality. From delicate butterflies to fierce superheroes, face paint enables children to transform themselves into the characters they admire. This personalization fosters a sense of empowerment and self-confidence.

2. Lasting Memories: Unlike balloon twisting, face painting leaves a lasting impression. Children can proudly wear their face paint throughout the event, showcasing their chosen designs and becoming walking works of art. The longevity of face paint allows for continued enjoyment and photo opportunities, making memories that can be cherished long after the event.

3. Adaptability and Detail: Face painting offers a wide range of design options, from simple motifs to intricate masterpieces. Skilled artists can bring any image or concept to life, incorporating fine details and vibrant colors. The versatility of face painting enables customization to suit individual preferences and event themes.

Cons of Face Painting:

1. Time and Patience: Creating elaborate face paint designs require time and patience. Face painters must work meticulously to achieve intricate details, which can lead to longer waiting times for children eager to have their faces painted. This may cause restlessness and impatience, especially in large groups or events with time constraints.

2. Skin Sensitivities and Allergies: Some children may have sensitive skin or allergies to certain face paint ingredients. Face painters must be diligent in selecting high-quality, hypoallergenic products and carefully assess any potential skin concerns before applying face paint. Proper hygiene and cleanliness are crucial to avoid any adverse reactions. Snazaroo, the paint that I use is hypoallergenic. I have only had one little girl out of thousands of kids, that said that the paint was burning her face.

Conclusion:

Balloon twisting and face painting offer distinct avenues for creativity and amusement in the world of children's entertainment. Balloon twisting provides immediate gratification, interactivity, and versatility, while face painting allows for personalized expression, lasting memories, and attention to detail. Each art form comes with its own set of pros and cons, and the choice between the two ultimately depends on the preferences, event dynamics, and safety considerations involved. Whatever the decision may be, both balloon twisting and face painting have the power to ignite the imagination and bring smiles to the faces of children, creating treasured moments that will be cherished for a lifetime.

CHAPTER 18:
EVERYDAY JOBS AND ADAPTIVE BEHAVIOR: THE SECRET TO EXCELLENT CUSTOMER SERVICE

In today's fast-paced and highly competitive business world, providing excellent customer service has become more critical than ever. Every interaction with a customer is an opportunity to create a lasting impression and build a loyal customer base. While companies invest heavily in training programs and customer service techniques, there is an often-overlooked source of expertise that can contribute significantly to delivering exceptional service: the experience gained from working everyday jobs.

1. Uncovering the Hidden Treasure:
   Everyday jobs are the ordinary tasks we encounter in our lives, ranging from part-time roles, summer jobs, or even household chores. These experiences, though seemingly mundane, possess the potential to cultivate valuable skills that can be applied to the realm of customer service. Each job, regardless of its nature, offers an opportunity to learn and develop essential qualities such as communication, empathy, problem-solving, and adaptability - all of which are fundamental to delivering exceptional customer experiences.

2. Communication as the Cornerstone:
   Effective communication lies at the heart of customer service. The ability to convey information clearly and understand the needs and expectations of customers can make or break a service interaction. Everyday jobs that involve direct communication, such as working as a waiter/waitress, call center agent, or even

a cashier, provide invaluable practice in mastering the art of effective communication. These experiences teach us to listen attentively, interpret non-verbal cues, and respond appropriately - skills that directly translate to providing personalized and empathetic customer service.

3. The Empathy Connection:
   Empathy, the ability to understand and share the feelings of another, is an indispensable skill when it comes to customer service. Empathetic interactions create a sense of trust and demonstrate genuine care for the customer's needs. Many everyday jobs offer opportunities to develop empathy, such as working as a nurse's aide, volunteer, or even as a babysitter. These roles expose individuals to diverse personalities and situations, fostering a deeper understanding of different perspectives and the ability to connect with customers on a human level.

4. Problem-Solving Prowess:
   Customer service often involves resolving issues and finding solutions to challenges. Everyday jobs that require problem-solving skills, such as being a handyman, IT support, or even a barista during the morning rush, sharpen one's ability to think on their feet and make decisions under pressure. These experiences cultivate resilience, adaptability, and resourcefulness - traits that enable customer service representatives to navigate complex situations with confidence and find innovative solutions that exceed customer expectations.

5. Adaptability in Action:
   In today's dynamic business landscape, adaptability is an indispensable quality. Everyday jobs teach us to adapt quickly to changing circumstances, whether it's dealing with unexpected situations or adjusting to the needs and preferences of different customers. Roles such as event planning, retail, or even delivery

driving require flexibility and the capacity to thrive in diverse environments. By leveraging the adaptability gained from such experiences, customer service professionals can seamlessly adjust their approach, accommodating each customer's unique requirements and ensuring a seamless experience.

6. The Power of Transferable Skills:
   Recognizing the value of the skills acquired from everyday jobs empowers individuals to leverage their unique experiences in the realm of customer service. By reflecting on the qualities they have developed, professionals can identify strengths and areas for improvement, ultimately enhancing their customer service performance. Organizations can also foster a culture that values diverse experiences, encouraging employees to share their backgrounds and learn from one another, creating a harmonious and customer-centric work environment.

7. Harnessing the Full Potential:
   To unlock the full potential of everyday job experiences, organizations must integrate these learning's into their training programs and talent development initiatives. By acknowledging the value of diverse backgrounds, organizations can tap into a rich pool of talent that brings a unique perspective to customer service.

CHAPTER 19:
APPRECIATING
RETURNING CUSTOMERS

Introduction: In the world of face painting, one of the most important aspects of success lies in building a strong and loyal customer base. Repeat customers are the lifeblood of any business, and it's essential to acknowledge and appreciate their continued support. In this chapter, we will explore various strategies for discounting returning customers and providing additional services to demonstrate our gratitude for their loyalty.

1. The Value of Returning Customers: Before delving into the ways we can appreciate returning customers, let's take a moment to understand the significance they hold for our business. Returning customers bring stability and consistency to our operations. Their continued patronage is a testament to the quality of our work and the positive experiences they've had in the past. By focusing on building long-term relationships, we can create a solid foundation for sustained growth and success.

2. Discount Programs: Discount programs are an effective way to show appreciation to returning customers while encouraging them to keep coming back. Here are a few ideas for implementing discount programs:

   a. Loyalty Cards: Introduce a loyalty card system where customers receive a stamp or signature for every face painting session they attend. After a certain number of visits, they can earn a free session or a discounted rate.

   b. Exclusive Membership: Create an exclusive membership program for returning customers, offering them exclusive perks such as discounted rates, priority booking, or early access to new designs and themes.

c. Referral Discounts: Encourage returning customers to refer their friends and family by offering them a discount on their next session for every successful referral. This not only rewards them for their loyalty but also helps expand your customer base.

3. Surprise Upgrades and Additional Services: Another way to express appreciation is by surprising returning customers with extra services or unexpected upgrades. These gestures can make them feel special and valued. Consider the following ideas:

a. Customized Designs: Take note of the designs and themes that returning customers particularly enjoy and surprise them with a personalized design or an upgrade to their favorite choice. This level of attentiveness shows that you value their preferences and are committed to going the extra mile.

b. Bonus Add-ons: Enhance the face painting experience by providing additional services or add-ons at no extra charge. It could be glitter accents, temporary tattoos, or even a small gift related to the chosen theme. These surprises create memorable moments that will leave a lasting impression.

c. VIP Treatment: Designate certain days or time slots exclusively for returning customers. Offer them priority booking, extended session times, or a dedicated area for their face painting experience. This VIP treatment reinforces their loyalty and makes them feel like valued members of your business.

Conclusion: Building and maintaining a loyal customer base is crucial for any successful face painting business. By implementing discount programs and providing additional services to appreciate returning customers, we reinforce their loyalty and ensure they keep coming back. These strategies not only strengthen our relationships with customers but also contribute to the growth and longevity of our business. Remember, a happy customer is not only a returning customer but also a potential ambassador for your face painting services, spreading positive word-of-mouth and attracting new clientele.

CHAPTER 20:
LESSONS LEARNED:
WHERE IS MY MONEY

As a freelancer or independent contractor, there are bound to be moments when the paychecks or payment doesn't arrive as expected. It's an unfortunate reality that many of us have faced at some point in our careers. In this chapter, I will share a personal experience of a time when I found myself in such a predicament and the valuable lessons I learned from it. Furthermore, I will provide you with practical advice on how to avoid similar situations in the future.

The anticipation of a payment can be both exciting and nerve-wracking. We work diligently, pouring our time, effort, and expertise into our projects, expecting fair compensation for our hard work. However, life often throws curveballs, and despite our best intentions, things don't always go according to plan.

I remember when I did a job for a retired marine. Everything was going smooth until it was time to pay. I told the couple the remaining balance and they sent the payment through Zelle. We used two different banks. They were with Navy Federal. The payment was never received. They showed me that they had sent the payment. I contacted my bank and also Zelle. To make a long story short, after going back and forward multiple times, my bank, Zelle, and Navy Federal said that it was nothing that they could do. I never got paid for the job.

I had another job the next day. The client sent the payment but it wasn't received immediately. I notified her and she was easier to deal with. She told me that it wasn't going through on her end as well, and to let her know so she could send it again. The payment went through later that day. She texted me to confirm that the payment was received. We both came to the conclusion that maybe it was something going on with Zelle that weekend. I still never received the payment from the Marine couple from the previous day.

From dealing with the Marine couple, I learned a lesson. At first, the project began smoothly, and I invested two hours perfecting every detail, and meeting my deadline with utmost professionalism. I believed that my hard work and dedication would guarantee a prompt payment. Unfortunately, reality had other plans.

Weeks turned into months, and I found myself eagerly checking my bank account each day, hoping to see a deposit that never came. My emails and calls to the client went unanswered, and frustration began to creep in. The promised compensation remained elusive, leaving me feeling deceived and disheartened.

I have not had any issues of this sort with Cashapp, Venmo, PayPal, Chime, and of course cash. The thing about Zelle, is if the money has been sent and it is not received immediately, then possibly it will be a loss for both parties.

Through this experience, I realized the importance of taking proactive measures to protect oneself from such situations. Here are some essential steps I've learned to help avoid similar issues in the future:

1. Clearly Define Terms: Before embarking on any project, ensure that you have a written contract or agreement that outlines all the relevant terms and conditions. (A written contract could also be the text message thread that was discussed. To be honest, if I were to hire a face painter and they asked me to sign a contract, I would probably just choose someone else.) This should include payment details, such as the agreed-upon rate, due dates, and any penalties for late payment. A well-defined contract serves as a reference point and a means of recourse if any payment-related issues arise.

2. Request an Upfront Payment or Deposit: Depending on the nature of the project, consider asking for an upfront payment or deposit to establish trust and demonstrate the client's commitment. This partial payment can help mitigate the risk of non-payment and act as a buffer against potential losses.

3. Establish a Clear Invoicing System: Implement an organized invoicing system that clearly states the services rendered, payment terms, and due dates. Make sure to follow up with reminders as the deadline approaches. Prompt and professional invoicing increases the likelihood of receiving timely payments.

4. Communicate Regularly: Maintain open lines of communication with your clients throughout the project. Regular updates, progress reports, and follow-up emails regarding invoices can serve as gentle reminders and help keep payment issues at bay. Consistent communication shows your professionalism and dedication, reminding clients of their obligation to compensate you fairly.

5. Escalate Issues Professionally: If a payment is delayed, approach the situation calmly and professionally. Begin by sending a polite reminder, allowing the client a chance to rectify the situation. If the problem persists, escalate your concerns to higher levels within the organization or seek legal advice if necessary. Remember, assertiveness is key when it comes to getting what you deserve.

6. Diversify Your Client Base: Relying on a single client for the bulk of your income can be risky. By diversifying your client base, you reduce the impact of non-payment from a single source. Seek out multiple projects or clients to ensure a steady cash flow and mitigate the consequences of delayed payments.

Reflecting on my own experience, I came to understand that despite taking precautions, there will always be instances where payment issues arise. However, by implementing these strategies, you can minimize the likelihood of encountering such problems and increase your chances of being compensated fairly and promptly.

Remember, as a freelancer or independent contractor, your skills and time are valuable. It is within your right to ensure that you receive appropriate compensation for your efforts. By setting clear expectations, maintaining open communication, and proactively addressing potential payment issues, you can navigate the world of freelancing with greater confidence and financial security.

CHAPTER 21:
EYES OF A CHILD

Have you ever noticed that, when you step out into the world with your face painting kit in tow, a strange phenomenon occurs? Suddenly, it feels as though you've become a magnet for curious stares from random kids and parents. You may find yourself wondering, "How do they know I'm a face painter?" It's as if they can sense your energy or have some kind of secret radar. Fear not, my fellow face painting enthusiast, for you are not alone. In this chapter, we will delve into the intriguing world of those captivating gazes and explore the reasons behind them.

Children possess an innate sense of wonder and curiosity. Their eyes are like little beacons of exploration, always seeking out new and fascinating things. And when they spot someone with the power to transform their faces into vibrant works of art, their natural curiosity takes over. It's almost as if they have an unspoken agreement among themselves to seek out face painters in a crowd. They recognize the artist within you, long before you've even picked up your brush.

The first thing to understand is that you emit a unique aura when you're carrying your face painting supplies. You radiate creativity, joy, and the promise of magical transformations. It's no wonder children are drawn to you like magnets! Your energy is contagious, and they can't help but be captivated by it.

Moreover, children are incredibly perceptive. They notice the slightest details, such as the twinkle in your eye when you see their face light up after a paint job, or the gentle smile that appears when you take a moment to appreciate their imaginative requests. Your passion for face painting shines through in every stroke, and they can feel it. They recognize the special connection you have with your art and are instinctively drawn to that spark within you.

But there's more to it than just your energy. Your appearance plays a role too. When you venture out into public spaces, you likely carry yourself with confidence, proudly displaying your face painting kit and the artistry you bring to the world. It's a visual cue that tells those around you that you're a face painter. Children, with their sharp eyes, pick up on these cues and understand what they mean.

So, next time you find yourself in a store or out in public, don't be surprised by the gazes of wonder. Embrace them! Allow yourself to be the source of intrigue and inspiration for those young, curious minds. Take it as a reminder of the magic you bring to their lives through your art.

To further engage with these inquisitive souls, you can use your interactions as an opportunity to share your passion. Talk to them, answer their questions, and maybe even offer a little sneak peek into the world of face painting. By fostering these connections, you can sow the seeds of creativity in the minds of future artists.

Every time I am at Target or out in public, I always have random kids looking at me. They range from the ages of one year to preteens. My wife will alert me of the child and I simply smile and wave. This opens up an opportunity for me to give the parent a card. Being a black male face painter, I sometimes show them photos because I know that I am not your normal idea of a face painter. This helps ease them and also prove that I am an experienced face painter and an opportunists.

I have always had a connection with kids that was unexplainable. Most crying babies or toddlers seem to find piece or comfort just by me picking them up and holding them since I was a kid. At times, the parents would even be surprised to their child's reaction. I had one parent that sat in my chair while holding her two year old daughter. She stated that her daughter would never be still, I performed my toddler test as stated in, "You're the Face Painter". It worked. She allowed me to paint her face with no fussing or fighting. The mother said, "Oh, my God. I am so calling you for her next birthday. I think it's your calm demeanor that she likes". She was a white woman attending a party of one of my previous white clients. I don't want to put a color on the example but it is also a message.

Remember, the gazes of random kids are not stares of judgment or scrutiny; they are the glimmers of possibility and admiration. So, hold your head high, wear your artist's badge proudly, and let those curious gazes be a testament to the transformative power of face painting. Embrace the magic that lies within you, and let it captivate the hearts of children everywhere.

Now, go forth and continue to paint the world with your imagination and creativity. Let the gazes of wonder be your guiding light as you embark on your face painting journey, spreading joy, and leaving a trail of smiles in your wake.

CHAPTER 22:
THE ART OF FACE PAINTING: WHERE CREATIVITY MEETS BUSINESS

In the realm of creative professions, face painting stands out as a unique blend of artistic expression and entrepreneurial endeavors. While it shares similarities with other jobs, face painting requires an exceptional set of skills, including cold selling, customer service, strategy, flexibility, and adaptability. In this chapter, we will explore how these qualities play an integral role in the world of face painting, allowing artists to transform their passion into a successful business venture.

1. The Power of Cold Selling Face painting, like many businesses, relies heavily on the art of cold selling. Whether it's at events, festivals, or parties, face painters must be skilled in approaching potential customers and enticing them with their artistry. It's not enough to wait for customers to come to you; face painters must actively seek opportunities to showcase their talents, often in high-traffic areas. By mastering the art of cold selling, face painters can attract a steady stream of clients and expand their business prospects.

2. Customer Service: Creating Memorable Experiences Beyond their creative abilities, face painters are in the business of creating memorable experiences. Each stroke of the brush is an opportunity to connect with customers and leave a lasting impression. Excellent customer service skills are crucial for understanding clients' needs, putting them at ease, and delivering a result that exceeds their expectations. Face painters must possess exceptional interpersonal skills, empathy, and the ability to work under pressure, ensuring that every interaction is enjoyable and rewarding for both the artist and the client.

3. Strategy: Balancing Artistic Vision and Practicality Successful face painters understand the importance of developing a strategic approach to their work. They must strike a delicate balance between their artistic vision and practicality. This involves carefully planning their designs, selecting appropriate materials, and managing time efficiently. Strategic thinking allows face painters to maximize their productivity, cater to a variety of clients' preferences, and ensure that their business operations run smoothly.

4. Flexibility: Adapting to Diverse Situations Face painters operate in a dynamic environment where each event and client presents unique challenges. They must be adaptable and flexible, ready to modify their designs or techniques to suit various themes, age groups, or time constraints. Whether faced with a child's request for a popular cartoon character or an adult's desire for an intricate tribal pattern, face painters must be able to pivot quickly, accommodating the client's wishes while maintaining their own artistic integrity.

5. Adaptability: Keeping Pace with Trends and Demands The world of face painting is ever-evolving, with trends and demands constantly shifting. Successful face painters remain updated with the latest styles, techniques, and popular characters, ensuring that they can meet the demands of their clientele. Staying adaptable allows them to stay relevant, attract new customers, and retain existing ones. This may involve attending workshops, collaborating with other artists, or actively engaging with the face painting community to share knowledge and stay abreast of industry developments.

6. Beyond the Brush: Business Acumen and Professionalism While face painting is undoubtedly a form of art, it is also a business. Face painters must develop a strong sense of business acumen, including financial management, marketing, branding, and networking. Building a reputable brand, establishing a loyal customer base, and forging partnerships with event organizers are all essential elements of a successful face painter.

CHAPTER 23:
UNVEILING THE
INTELLECTUAL CANVAS

Introduction:

As face painters, we often marvel at the endless possibilities that come to life on the human canvas. The strokes of a brush and the swirls of vibrant colors bring joy, wonder, and excitement to both the artist and the wearer. But beneath the surface of this creative art form lies a realm of intellectual property waiting to be explored. In this chapter, we will delve into the fascinating world of face painting and discover the intellectual riches that can be gained from this expressive and captivating experience.

The Artistic Expression:

Face painting, at its core, is an art form that thrives on artistic expression. It provides a platform for artists to showcase their creativity, imagination, and unique style. Each stroke of the brush carries a piece of the artist's individuality and reflects their personal artistic vision. In this sense, the face becomes a living canvas, allowing for the creation of awe-inspiring designs that can leave a lasting impression. This is how the muscle memory is created.

Trademarks and Branding:

In the world of face painting, some artists develop unique styles or signature designs that become synonymous with their brand. These distinctive elements can be protected through trademarks, which allow artists to establish their identity in the market. By registering a trademark for their logo, name, or distinctive design, face painters can build a recognizable brand that sets them apart from competitors. This not only strengthens their market presence but also safeguards their intellectual property from being exploited by others. My aim is to inspire others, so using my design as a base and putting a twist on it to create their own is very welcomed. This happens all the time with canvas art.

Educational Resources:

Face painting is not only about creating stunning designs but also about sharing knowledge and expertise with others. Artists who have developed unique techniques or mastered specific styles can create educational resources, such as books, tutorials, or online courses. These resources not only contribute to the growth and development of the face painting community but also serve as intellectual property assets that can generate income for the artist. This is why I wrote this book.

Collaborations and Cross-Pollination:

The world of face painting is filled with opportunities for collaboration and cross-pollination of ideas. Artists can join forces with other creative professionals, such as photographers, makeup artists, or event organizers, to create unforgettable experiences. Collaborative projects often lead to the creation of new intellectual property, as the fusion of different artistic talents gives rise to innovative designs, techniques, and approaches. If you don't want to limit your money, you can do body paints for models and exotic dancers. One must stay professional at all times or this could ruin your reputation.

Conclusion:

Beyond the enchantment of colors and designs, face painting offers a wealth of intellectual property opportunities for artists. From copyright protection to trademarks, licensing, educational resources, and collaborations, face painters can unlock the full potential of their artistic expression. By recognizing and harnessing these opportunities, artists can not only safeguard their creative work but also reap the rewards of their intellectual endeavors, ensuring a vibrant and flourishing face painting community for years to come.

CHAPTER 24:
THE RARE ARTISTRY

In a world filled with vibrant colors and imaginative designs, the art of face painting is a cherished craft that brings joy and wonder to people of all ages. It is a form of expression that transcends language barriers and cultural boundaries, allowing artists to create living, breathing works of art on the canvas of human faces. Yet, within this diverse realm, there exists a rarity that adds an extra layer of enchantment—the black male face painter.

Throughout history, black artists have faced numerous challenges and barriers in various artistic disciplines. From painters and sculptors to musicians and actors, their journeys have been marked by struggle and resilience. The world of face painting is no exception. This mesmerizing art form, often associated with childhood innocence, has been predominantly dominated by white female artists. The scarcity of black male face painters is a testament to the intricate tapestry of societal norms and expectations.

The rarity of black male face painters stems from a multitude of factors, both historical and cultural. In the early days of face painting's popularity, societal stereotypes and limited opportunities hindered the growth and representation of black artists. The absence of role models and lack of encouragement meant that aspiring black male artists rarely pursued this particular form of artistic expression. Additionally, the societal perception of face painting as a feminine pursuit further discouraged black men from exploring their creative talents in this medium.

However, in recent years, as the world continues to evolve and break free from the shackles of stereotypes, there has been a growing movement to diversify the face painting industry. I am one exceptionally talented black male artist that has emerged, showcasing my extraordinary skills and breathing new life into the art form. My presence not only challenges the prejudgment surrounding face painting but also serves as a source of inspiration for aspiring artists from all backgrounds.

The unique perspective that a black male face painter can bring to his craft is an invaluable asset. My artistic journey often draws from personal experiences, cultural heritage, and a profound understanding of the power of representation. The strokes of my brushes tell stories that resonate deeply with people of color, providing a sense of belonging and pride. Through their intricate designs and expert technique, I create a visual tapestry that celebrates diversity and challenges the conventional norms of the industry.

The rarity of black male face painter has become a source of fascination, drawing attention and intrigue wherever I perform. My artistry is not merely confined to transforming a blank canvas into a vivid spectacle of color and imagination. It serves as a vehicle for storytelling, empowerment, and connection—a testament to the resilience and creativity of individuals who have defied the odds and defied societal expectations.

As the world continues to embrace the beauty of diversity and inclusivity, it is crucial to uplift and celebrate the work of black male face painters. Their contributions to the art form transcend boundaries, bridging the gaps between cultures and fostering a deeper understanding of our shared humanity. Through their remarkable talent and unwavering dedication, these artists are rewriting the narrative, proving that creativity knows no boundaries and that true artistry lies in the heart and soul of the artist, regardless of their gender or ethnicity.

In the world of face painting, the convergence of artistic talent and business skills is what sets apart the exceptional artists. By embracing cold selling, mastering customer service, developing strategic thinking, staying flexible and adaptable, and nurturing their business acumen, face painters can transform their passion into a fulfilling and thriving profession. With each brushstroke, they create not only beautiful designs but also unforgettable experiences for their clients, leaving a colorful mark in their journey as both artists and entrepreneurs. Bottom line, I'm making face painting cool.

CHAPTER 25:
PARTY TIME

In this chapter, we'll explore the art of transforming faces into stunning works of art, and delve into the fascinating realm of face painting rates, along with the most requested options among face painting, bounce houses, balloon twisting, and clowns.

Rates of Cost:

When it comes to face painting services, rates can vary depending on several factors such as location, the experience of the artist, event duration, and the intricacy of the designs requested. Generally, face painting services are priced per hour or per face. Here are a few examples of typical face painting rates:

1. Hourly Rate: Many professional face painters charge an hourly rate, which usually ranges from $50 to $150 per hour. This rate often includes all necessary supplies and a wide selection of design options for participants to choose from.

2. Per Face Rate: Some face painters charge per face, with rates ranging from $5 to $20 per face. This approach allows clients to have a set budget and provides an estimate based on the number of attendees who wish to be painted.

Most Requested Options:

While face painting is an incredibly popular choice, it's worth exploring other entertainment options that often complement face painting services. Here are a few of the most requested options in addition to face painting:

1. Bounce Houses: Bounce houses are a fantastic addition to any event, particularly for children's parties. They provide hours of entertainment, allowing kids to jump, slide, and have a blast in

a safe and supervised environment. Bounce house rental rates typically range from $100 to $300 for a few hours, depending on the size and complexity of the structure.

2. Balloon Twisting: Balloon twisting is another crowd-pleaser that goes hand-in-hand with face painting. Talented balloon artists can create intricate balloon sculptures and designs, captivating the imagination of both children and adults. Balloon twisting rates can range from $75 to $150 per hour, depending on the complexity of the requested designs.

3. Clowns: Clowns bring joy, laughter, and a touch of magic to any event. Whether it's through balloon animals, silly tricks, or comedic performances, clowns are a classic choice for entertainment. Rates for professional clowns typically range from $150 to $300 per hour, depending on their experience and the scope of their performance.

Remember, these rates are general estimates, and it's always best to consult with local service providers or event planners to get accurate pricing based on your specific needs. At the end of the day, face paint smears, balloons pop, bounce houses deflate, and clowns are creepy.

In conclusion, face painting opens the door to a world of imagination and creativity. With its wide range of design options and the ability to bring smiles to faces of all ages, it remains a beloved choice for parties, festivals, and events. When combined with other popular options such as bounce houses, balloon twisting, and clowns, it creates an unforgettable experience that will leave your guests with cherished memories for years to come. So, dive into the world of face painting, let your imagination soar, and create a truly colorful and captivating event!

CHAPTER 26:
PRICING AND CREATING PACKAGES

Introduction:

Face painting is a delightful art form that brings joy to people of all ages. As a professional face painter, it's essential to establish clear pricing structures and create attractive packages for your clients. In this chapter, we'll explore the various factors to consider when determining your pricing and guide you in creating appealing packages that cater to different customer needs.

Set Your Prices:

Determining the right price for your face painting services requires a balance between covering your costs, reflecting your expertise, and remaining competitive in the market. Consider the following factors when setting your prices:

1. Time and Complexity: The duration and intricacy of each face painting design should influence your pricing. Intricate designs or those requiring additional details and special effects may warrant a higher fee.

2. Experience and Skill: Your level of expertise and the quality of your work should be reflected in your pricing. As you gain more experience and build a reputation, you can adjust your prices accordingly.

3. Materials and Supplies: Factor in the cost of face paints, brushes, sponges, glitters, and other materials you use. Keep track of your expenses to ensure they are covered by your pricing.

4. Overheads: Consider any additional costs associated with your business, such as travel expenses, insurance, marketing, and booth rentals, if applicable.

5. Local Market: Research the prices charged by other face painters in your area to get an idea of the prevailing rates. While you should remain competitive, don't undervalue your skills and time.

Create Packages:

Offering packages allows you to provide a variety of options to your clients and simplifies the decision-making process for them. Here's how you can create appealing packages:

1. Basic Package: Start with a basic package that includes simple designs suitable for children's parties or community events. This package can have a fixed price and a limited selection of designs.

2. Deluxe Package: Create a more comprehensive package for larger events or occasions that require more elaborate designs. This package could include a wider range of designs, glitter or special effects, and personalized options. Set the price higher than the basic package to account for the additional time and materials.

3. Theme-based Packages: Consider creating theme-based packages tailored to specific events or holidays. For example, you could offer packages for Halloween, Christmas, or sports-themed parties. These packages should include designs related to the theme and may have special pricing or added value.

4. Add-On Options: Provide add-on options that customers can choose to enhance their face painting experience. These can include options like glitter tattoos, gem embellishments, or face painting workshops for larger groups.

5. Custom Packages: If a client has unique requirements or a specific budget, be flexible in creating custom packages that suit their needs. This demonstrates your willingness to accommodate their preferences and can lead to repeat business and positive referrals.

Package Pricing Considerations:

When determining prices for your packages, take into account the following factors:

- Time: Estimate how long each package will take to complete and factor in the hourly rate you wish to earn. Adjust prices accordingly for longer or more intricate designs.

- Materials: Consider the cost of materials and supplies specific to each package. For example, if a package includes the use of specialty face paints or glitters, account for the additional expenses.

- Value: Assess the overall value of each package by comparing it to individual pricing. Offer a slight discount or added value to make the package more appealing than booking individual services.

Conclusion:

Pricing your face painting services appropriately and creating attractive packages is vital for your business's success. Consider the time, complexity, experience, and market factors when setting your prices. One should craft packages that cater to different customer needs, offering options for both basic and deluxe designs, theme-based events, and add-on services. Regularly review and adjust your pricing and packages to remain competitive in the market and reflect your growing expertise as a face painter.

CHAPTER 27:
EMBRACING FEEDBACK AND GROWING AS AN ARTIST

Introduction:

As a face painter, one of the most valuable skills you can develop is the ability to accept criticism and feedback on your work. While it can be difficult to hear someone critique your creations, learning to embrace feedback is essential for your growth and improvement as an artist. In this chapter, we will explore the importance of accepting criticism, understanding different types of feedback, and utilizing it to enhance your face painting skills. So, let's dive in and discover how feedback can be your greatest teacher.

1. The Power of Feedback:
   Feedback is a powerful tool that can provide you with fresh perspectives, new ideas, and valuable insights into your work. It offers an opportunity for growth and helps you identify areas where you can improve. Remember, feedback is not a personal attack on your abilities but rather a means to elevate your skills and expand your artistic horizons.

2. Differentiating between Constructive Criticism and Destructive Comments:
   Not all feedback is created equal. It's crucial to understand the difference between constructive criticism and destructive comments. Constructive criticism is thoughtful, specific, and focuses on the improvement of your work. It provides actionable suggestions and points out areas that need attention. Destructive comments, on the other hand, are negative, unhelpful, and lack substance. Learning to distinguish between the two will allow

you to filter out unproductive feedback and focus on what truly benefits your growth.

3. The Art of Receiving Feedback:
   Receiving feedback gracefully is a skill that every artist should cultivate. Here are some tips to help you navigate the feedback process effectively:

   a. Cultivate an Open Mind: Approach feedback with an open and receptive mindset. Be willing to listen and consider different perspectives on your work.

   b. Separate Emotion from Evaluation: Try not to take feedback personally. Instead, view it as an opportunity for improvement. Remember, feedback is about your art, not your worth as an artist.

   c. Ask for Clarification: If the feedback you receive is unclear or vague, don't hesitate to ask for more specific details. This will help you understand the critique better and apply it appropriately.

   d. Take Time to Reflect: After receiving feedback, take some time to reflect on the suggestions and insights provided. Consider how you can incorporate them into your future work and what lessons you can learn from them.

4. Applying Feedback:
   Once you have received feedback, it's important to apply it effectively. Here's how you can make the most of the feedback you receive:

   a. Analyze and Prioritize: Evaluate the feedback you have received and identify the areas that resonate with you the most. Determine which suggestions align with your artistic vision and prioritize them for implementation.

b. Experiment and Practice: Use the feedback as a guide for experimentation and practice. Incorporate the suggested changes into your work and observe how they impact your technique and final results.

c. Seek Additional Input: Consider seeking feedback from a diverse group of people, including fellow face painters, mentors, or even your clients. Multiple perspectives can offer valuable insights and help you refine your skills further.

5. The Growth Mindset:
   Embracing feedback is part of adopting a growth mindset—an attitude that allows you to continuously learn, adapt, and improve. Understand that every artist, regardless of their skill level, can benefit from constructive criticism and feedback. Embrace the journey of growth, and remember that feedback is an opportunity to become a better face painter.

Conclusion:

Accepting criticism and feedback with an open mind is a crucial aspect of an artist's journey. Embracing feedback empowers you to expand your creative boundaries, refine your techniques, and grow as a face painter. Remember, each critique is a chance to evolve, so welcome feedback with open arms, apply it thoughtfully, and watch your artistry soar to new heights.

CHAPTER 28:
THE LINE-UP DILEMMA

If I am the only face painter and there is more than 20 kids at a party, I cannot keep the position of the kids in line. I paint what sits down in my chair. I may get a glimpse of the second and third kid in line, but my main focus is the face that I'm working on.

I have been in situations where the parents start to argue about what child is next and how long the child has been waiting. We have been waiting thirty minutes; well we've been waiting almost an hour. I break the ice by saying; well I've been here since 12:40 PM.

If a kid cries, of course no one wants to see it, but to be honest as well; no one wants to hear it either. Everyone is waiting and the kids have to learn patience. I don't do the 2 minute stencil paint or the half face masks. This is one reason that I stand out from the rest, which I hear a lot from my clients and their kids. To produce what the kid's unlimited imaginations create, it takes about 5 to 7 minutes.

Also, not all kids are able to sit still like a statue. I have had two year olds be more still than a twelve year old. I have had adults be the most difficult faces to paint at times. All of the movement can slow down the progress of completing the face. To be sure that I give the client great quality at an affordable cost, I try to work with the problematic customers and create everlasting memories.

So, parents don't argue and fight because of whose next. Stand in line with your child if they are not big enough to keep the order of the line. I can't be the face painter, referee, and babysitter. But again, I thank you for being patient, and who's next?

CHAPTER 29:
CREATING YOUR OWN HASHTAG

Introduction:

In the age of social media, showcasing your face painting skills has become easier than ever before. By harnessing the power of hashtags, you can create a digital gallery of your work and connect with a vast audience of enthusiasts, clients, and fellow artists. In this chapter, we'll explore the art of crafting your own unique hashtag, providing you with an automatic way to share and promote your face painting creations. Let's dive in and unlock the potential of social media to elevate your artistry!

Section 1: The Power of Hashtags

Hashtags have transformed the way we discover content and connect with like-minded individuals across various social media platforms. By appending a hashtag to your posts, you categorize them under a specific topic or theme, making it easier for people to find your work. The beauty of hashtags lies in their ability to create a virtual art gallery, enabling anyone interested in face painting to explore your creations with a single click.

Section 2: Crafting Your Unique Hashtag

1. Reflect Your Style: Consider your artistic style and personality when creating a hashtag. You want it to be a representation of your unique identity as a face painter. Think about words or phrases that encapsulate your approach, such as #ipaintlovethekids, #yourkidsfavoritefacepainter, or #yourethefacepainter.

2. Be Memorable: Your hashtag should be easy to remember and spell. Avoid overly complex or obscure terms that might confuse your audience. Aim for simplicity and clarity, ensuring that anyone who comes across your hashtag can recall it effortlessly.

3. Research Existing Hashtags: Before settling on a hashtag, take some time to research its availability and popularity. Check different social media platforms to see if your chosen hashtag already exists or if it is widely associated with unrelated content. You want your hashtag to be unique to your work, so consider adding your name or initials to make it more distinctive, such as #ipaintbytaj or #tajmarkale.

4. Short and Sweet: Keeping your hashtag concise is crucial. Longer hashtags can be difficult to read, remember, and can eat up valuable characters in your social media captions. Aim for brevity without sacrificing the essence of your artistic style.

5. Consistency Is Key: Once you've settled on a hashtag, be consistent in its usage across your social media platforms. Incorporate it into your captions, comments, and even your profile bio. By using it consistently, you create a recognizable brand identity and establish a connection with your audience.

Section 3: Maximizing Hashtag Exposure

1. Strategic Placement: When posting your face painting photos, strategically place your hashtag within the caption or comment section to ensure visibility. Consider placing it at the end of your caption or separating it with line breaks to make it stand out.

2. Cross-Platform Promotion: Extend the reach of your hashtag by sharing your posts on multiple platforms simultaneously. Connect your Instagram, Facebook, Twitter, and other relevant accounts to ensure your face painting creations are visible to a broader audience.

3. Engage with the Community: Explore other face painters' work by following relevant hashtags. Engaging with their posts, leaving thoughtful comments, and sharing your own creations under the same hashtags can help you build connections, gain exposure, and inspire others to do the same.

4. Collaborate and Tag: Collaborate with fellow face painters or models and use your hashtag when posting collaborative projects. This cross-promotion exposes your work to new audiences and strengthens your network within the face painting community.

Conclusion:

Creating your own unique hashtag is a powerful tool for showcasing your face painting skills and connecting with a passionate audience. By following the tips outlined in this chapter, you'll establish a digital footprint that allows others to discover, admire, and appreciate your artistic journey. Embrace the world of hashtags, unleash your creativity, and watch as your face painting creations become part of a thriving online community. Happy hashtagging!

I was born in the 80's, so when I was growing up the hashtag was known as a pound sign. To stay connected to this day and age, I created my hashtags. You can view my work by selecting the following hashtags: #ipaintbytaj; #Ipaintlovethekids; #ipaintworld; #yourethefacepainter; #yourneighborsfavoritefacepainter; #yourkidsfavoritefacepainter; #tajmarkale; and #yourfavoritefacepainter.

CHAPTER 30:
UNLEASHING THE IMAGINATION:
THE ARTISTRY OF CHILDHOOD

As artists, we often seek inspiration from the world around us. We search for those magical moments, the fleeting glimpses of beauty and wonder that ignite our creativity. And while many find inspiration in nature, landscapes, or profound emotions, there is a wellspring of untapped inspiration waiting within the realm of childhood.

Children possess a unique lens through which they view the world—a lens unfiltered by the burdens of adulthood. Their imaginations run wild, fueled by boundless curiosity and an innate ability to see the extraordinary in the ordinary. As artists, we have much to learn from these pint-sized visionaries, and interacting with our kids and young family members can reveal a treasure trove of artistic possibilities.

When we engage with children, we enter a realm of untamed creativity and unbounded exploration. Their uninhibited spirits and uninformed perspectives inspire us to look beyond what we know, to embrace the unfamiliar, and to reconnect with the simplicity and purity of the artistic process. In their presence, we shed the weight of preconceived notions and self-imposed limitations, allowing us to dive headfirst into the boundless sea of imagination.

One of the most powerful lessons children teach us is the art of seeing with fresh eyes. They notice details we often overlook, whether it's the intricate patterns on a butterfly's wings, the vibrant hues of a sunset, or the shapes created by clouds in the sky. Through their innocent observations, they remind us of the beauty that surrounds us every day, waiting to be captured on canvas.

As artists, we tend to grow comfortable with our preferred subjects, our tried-and-true techniques. But children push us out of our artistic comfort zones, encouraging us to experiment and take risks. They urge us to paint with abandon, to mix colors without hesitation, and to embrace the unexpected results. In their world, there are no mistakes, only happy accidents waiting to be transformed into something marvelous. I learn a lot of new characters from interacting with my kids.

Interacting with children also introduces us to the art of storytelling. Kids possess a natural inclination to weave narratives, creating imaginary worlds and characters that come to life before our eyes. By listening to their tales, we learn the importance of narrative in art, how to convey emotions and messages through our chosen mediums. We discover that our paintings can become windows into captivating stories, capturing the essence of a moment and inviting viewers to step into a different reality.

Moreover, children ignite our sense of playfulness, which is often forgotten in the seriousness of adulthood. Their unrestrained joy and laughter remind us that art is not solely about the final masterpiece but also about the process of creation. They teach us to embrace the messiness, to revel in the act of painting itself, and to let go of self-judgment. In their presence, we reconnect with the sheer delight of wielding a brush or molding clay, finding solace in the act of bringing our inner visions to life.

In the end, engaging with our kids and young family members goes beyond teaching us what to paint; it teaches us how to see, how to play, and how to let our creativity run free. Through their unencumbered perspectives, we tap into a limitless reservoir of inspiration and rekindle the flame of our artistic spirit. As we embrace the wonder of childhood, our art takes on new life—a vibrant testament to the beauty and brilliance that resides within us all.

So, let us step into the realm of childhood, hand in hand with our little muses, and embark on a journey of boundless creativity, where the wonders of the world unfold before our eyes, and our brushes dance with the magic of youthful imagination.

CHAPTER 31:
BALANCING ART AND FAMILY

As an aspiring face painter, there's no doubt that you possess an incredible talent and a passion for bringing smiles to people's faces. The joy you bring to children and adults alike is immeasurable, and your artistic skills continue to grow with each stroke of the brush. However, there is a price to pay for dedicating yourself to this craft. Face painting can often demand a significant amount of time, especially on weekends when parties and events are most prevalent. This reality can inevitably result in a sacrifice of family time, leaving you torn between pursuing your passion and being present for your loved ones.

In this chapter, we will explore the challenges faced by face painters who have to strike a balance between their artistic endeavors and their family obligations. While it is true that success in the face painting industry often requires attending parties and events on weekends, it is essential to navigate these commitments while ensuring your family remains a priority.

When you first embark on your face painting journey, you might find yourself overwhelmed by the demands of building a client base and establishing your reputation. Parties and events will occupy a considerable portion of your weekends, leaving you with limited time to spend with your family. Balancing these commitments is crucial, as neglecting your loved ones for the sake of your career can have long-lasting effects on your relationships.

To begin reconciling these competing demands, open communication with your family is essential. Explain to them your passion for face painting and the opportunities it brings, while also acknowledging the time commitment required. Encourage an open dialogue, allowing your loved ones to express their concerns and needs. Together, you can establish boundaries and find compromises that work for everyone involved.

One strategy to strike a balance is to set aside specific days or hours during the week that are dedicated solely to family time. Create rituals and traditions that become treasured moments for all, reinforcing the bond between you and your loved ones. By making the most of the time you do have together, you can strengthen your relationships and create lasting memories that will withstand the busyness of your face painting career.

Additionally, consider involving your family in your face painting endeavors whenever possible. Organize events where your loved ones can assist you, allowing them to be part of the creative process and share in the joy of bringing happiness to others. By incorporating your family into your passion, you not only create meaningful experiences but also teach them valuable lessons about dedication, creativity, and the importance of pursuing one's dreams.

As you navigate the challenges of balancing face painting and family life, remember that self-care is equally crucial. Taking care of your own physical and mental well-being will enable you to be present and engaged in both aspects of your life. Find moments for relaxation, engage in hobbies outside of face painting, and prioritize your own needs. By replenishing your own energy, you can better fulfill the demands of your career and maintain a harmonious family life.

Ultimately, finding a healthy equilibrium between your face painting career and your family will require ongoing effort, communication, and flexibility. Recognize that there will be periods when your face painting commitments will take precedence, but strive to balance them with quality time spent with your loved ones. Embrace the moments when you can be fully present with your family, cherishing the love and support they provide as you pursue your artistic passion.

I try to make up for my absence sometimes by using the money that I've made for a party or two that day, and take my family out for a good time when I get home. Even when I am out, I still try to pass out cards to families and gain new potential customers. In the end, I am thinking of my family and they are the ones that I do it for.

I have explained to my kids why I do what I do, and assure them that I will make it up to them. As soon as I arrive home, my two younger sons, Christian age 10 and Camron age 5, meet me at the door and take anything out of my hands that I may have. I then receive hugs and a dog with a wagging tail placing her paws on my thighs. If my wife is not cooking, then she too will be looking to see what I have brought home to eat. We then enjoy the rest of the night as a family night sitting in the living room. We usually unite by watching movies and eating popcorn, playing Mario Kart 8, building with Lego's, working a puzzle, or wrestling with each other.

Remember that your family is your foundation, and their understanding and support are invaluable. With open communication, mutual respect, and a commitment to maintaining a harmonious balance, you can navigate the challenges of face painting while still nurturing the relationships that mean the most to you.

CHAPTER 32:
PROFESSIONALISM AND BOUNDARIES IN FACE PAINTING

In the world of face painting, it's essential to maintain a high level of professionalism when working with clients, regardless of their gender. As a black male face painter, it is important to address a particular aspect of professionalism - maintaining appropriate boundaries with female clients. In this chapter, we will delve into the significance of professionalism, establishing boundaries, and provide practical tips on how to ensure a comfortable and respectful environment for everyone involved.

The Importance of Professionalism: Professionalism is the cornerstone of any successful face painting business. It not only sets you apart as a skilled artist but also fosters trust and confidence in your abilities. When clients hire you, they expect a professional experience that goes beyond just artistic skills. Professionalism encompasses how you conduct yourself, communicate, and interact with your clients.

Respect Boundaries: Boundaries are vital in any professional relationship, and they play an even more significant role when working with female clients. It is crucial to understand that your role as a face painter is not to flirt or engage in seductive behavior. Such actions can undermine your professionalism, make clients uncomfortable, and potentially harm your reputation. By maintaining clear boundaries, you create a safe and respectful environment where clients can fully enjoy the face painting experience.

Tips for Staying Professional: Here are some practical tips to help you stay professional and maintain appropriate boundaries with female clients:

1. Set the Tone: From the moment you begin interacting with clients, establish a professional and respectful tone. Greet them warmly,

maintain eye contact, and speak in a friendly but neutral manner. This sets the foundation for a professional working relationship.

2. Focus on the Art: During the face painting process, direct your attention to your craft. Concentrate on creating stunning designs and executing your skills to the best of your ability. Keep conversations centered on the artwork or general topics related to the event, such as the theme or occasion.

3. Maintain Personal Space: Respect personal space boundaries by keeping an appropriate distance when interacting with clients. Avoid physical contact unless necessary for the face painting process, and always ask for consent before doing so.

4. Use Appropriate Language: Be mindful of the language you use when speaking to female clients. Avoid making comments that could be interpreted as flirtatious or inappropriate. Focus on maintaining a professional tone and engaging in conversations that are respectful and inclusive.

5. Handle Compliments Gracefully: It's natural for clients to appreciate your work and express their admiration. When receiving compliments, thank them graciously and redirect the conversation back to their experience or the face painting itself. Avoid responding in a way that may be interpreted as flirtatious or suggestive.

6. Seek Feedback: Regularly ask for feedback from clients to gauge their satisfaction with your services. This shows that you value their opinion and are committed to delivering the best possible experience. Take feedback seriously, address any concerns promptly, and continuously strive to improve your professionalism. I sometimes ask for client's phone numbers when I meet them on Facebook or Instagram because it will be easier to keep up with the conversation. In your phone, the most recent text are always at the top of your log. You can forget about a person if they are not one of your usual contacts. I remind them that I am a professional,

and I will send screenshots of my list of clients and let them see how many people that I have worked with.

In conclusion, maintaining professionalism and respecting boundaries is crucial for any face painter, regardless of gender or background. As a black male face painter, it is important to navigate these dynamics with sensitivity and professionalism. By setting a professional tone, focusing on the art, respecting personal space, using appropriate language, gracefully handling compliments, and seeking feedback, you can ensure a comfortable and respectful experience for all your clients. Remember, professionalism is the key to building a successful and respected face painting career.

CHAPTER 33:
CONCLUSION

When I say "black male face painter," it may initially conjure up a specific image in your mind: a talented artist, perhaps an individual of African descent, embracing their passion for face painting. But let us delve deeper into the true meaning behind these words and unravel the tapestry of possibilities they represent.

In a world that has often adhered to conventional norms, it is only natural for certain occupations and art forms to be attributed to a particular group or gender. Face painting, too, has been shaped by such assumptions, with the notion that it primarily belonged to a certain archetype—females or individuals of a different ethnicity, for instance. However, as the world around us evolves, it becomes clear that the confines of such stereotypes are crumbling, giving rise to a rich mosaic of diversity.

The essence of face painting lies not in the gender, ethnicity, or background of the artist, but rather in the limitless potential to transform, create, and celebrate the human face. By broadening our perspective, we open ourselves to a world of fresh possibilities, where artists of all backgrounds, experiences, and identities converge to redefine the face painting landscape.

When we break free from the limitations of stereotypes, we find that artistry knows no boundaries. A face painter can be anyone—regardless of gender, race, or background—who possesses a passion for the craft, an eye for detail, and a heart eager to bring joy to others. It is the shared love for this art form that unites us, transcending superficial differences and fostering a sense of community that celebrates our unique abilities.

Imagine a vibrant face painting festival, where artists from diverse walks of life gather, each contributing their own style, techniques, and cultural influences. A harmonious blend of talent, a kaleidoscope of colors, and an atmosphere brimming with inclusivity—the true spirit of face painting emerges, breaking down barriers, and dispelling preconceived notions.

As society progresses towards a more inclusive future, we have the responsibility to challenge the status quo, to create spaces where all artists feel welcome and celebrated. By recognizing the universal nature of face painting, we can empower individuals who may not conform to the traditional expectations of this craft to express themselves freely, encouraging innovation and nurturing a more dynamic art form.

I had one little girl ask for a fox unicorn. I thought that this was so unique. I mean, it was a first for me. As I was talking to the hiring client on the phone, I told him about the fox unicorn. He laughed and stated that, it was his daughter that requested it. He told me how much that he appreciated me and that everyone loved my work. They assured me that I would be back next year. I include this experience because it reminds me of how rare I am to the industry. I am a unicorn in the face painting world. So I created a world, iPAINT World. Welcome, to iPAINT's world.

So, the next time you encounter the phrase "black male face painter," remember that it represents so much more than a simple description. It symbolizes the evolution of an art form, a testament to the human spirit's boundless creativity, and an invitation to explore the vast possibilities that lie beyond conventional boundaries.

Let us embrace this shift and celebrate the diverse faces behind the brushes, recognizing that true beauty emerges when we open our hearts and minds to the full spectrum of human experience. In doing so, we elevate face painting to new heights, infusing it with the richness and diversity it deserves.

Together, let us paint a world where every artist, regardless of their gender, ethnicity, or background, can unleash their creativity and make a lasting impact—one brushstroke at a time. iPaintbyTaj.